PREPARING STUDENTS FOR THE 21ST CENTURY

S0-BXX-507

By Donna Uchida
with Marvin Cetron and Floretta McKenzie

AMERICAN ASSOCIATION OF SCHOOL ADMINISTRATORS

Table of Contents

Math, logic, and reasoning; interpersonal skills; information accessing and processing using technology; writing skills; history and government knowledge; multicultural understanding, including knowledge of foreign languages and world geography, an integrated curriculum

Oral and written communication; critical thinking, reasoning, and problem-solving; self-discipline; computers; job success; adaptability and flexibility; conflict resolution and negotiation; interpreting and applying data; knowledge of other languages; reading and understanding

Honesty and practicing the golden rule; respect for the value of effort; appreciating diversity; working as a team member; being responsible for one's own actions; being committed to family, personal, and community life; resolving disagreements

Preface

We stand on the edge of a new millennium. Not since the year 1000 has anyone been able to make that claim.

John Dewey referred to education as the engine that drives our society. That is why education is so important and why it generates such intense discussion—even controversy. Most of us have been to school and we have opinions on how schools should operate and what they should teach.

As we approach the 21st century, it's time to rev up the engines of education. The future of our free and democratic society and our free-market economy depend on it. So do the individual futures of millions of children, who will need to live fulfilling lives, serve as good citizens, and contribute to our economy.

In undertaking this historic project, the American Association of School Administrators called upon the expertise and opinions of more than 50 leaders in education, business, and government. They were asked to address what students would need to know and be able to do and the behaviors they would need to exhibit to thrive during the next century.

Responses were enlightening. While most agree that math and science and other core subjects are essential, they also believe that civility and ethical behavior must guide today's children and youth, now and in their adult futures. Our panel, which responded to a three-round quasi-Delphi process, also had important things to say to school leaders, parents, business and professional people, and representatives of government about the roles they need to play if our schools and our children are to be successful.

Preparing Students for the 21st Century is not intended to be the last word about what schools need to teach or how they or their constituents need to change. It is intended to stir discussions about the needs of today's students and their schools as we approach the turn of the century. In short, putting life into the dynamic ideas expressed in this book will depend on people like you, whatever your walk of life.

The American Association of School Administrators, founded in 1865, has always been an advocate for children and youth. Our aims include improving the condition of our children, helping prepare schools for the 21st century, connecting schools and communities, and enhancing school leadership.

I wish you happy reading and stimulating discussions.

Paul D. Houston
Executive Director
American Association of School Administrators

ntroduction

"There is nothing like a dream to create the future," wrote Victor Hugo many years ago. The beginning of a new millennium is the time to determine just what that dream should be as we prepare children to thrive in the 21st century. We have a choice—we can be overcome by whatever the future brings, or we can help shape it.

Some hard questions demanding answers, or at the very least, sound and concentrated attention, include:

➡ What should we be doing today to prepare children for the 21st century?

➡ What will children need to know?

➡ What behaviors and skills will be important?

➡ How might educators, citizens, parents, business, and government contribute to children's success?

In looking for answers to these questions, we didn't gaze into any crystal balls, but instead asked a panel of distinguished experts throughout America who were willing to participate in our Council of 55. These 55 advisers, from such fields as education, business, government, psychology, sociology, anthropology, demography, and others, were asked to name the most important knowledge, skills, and behaviors students will need to exhibit if they are to prosper in the 21st century.

This book is based on the results of the study, and on the views of this sample of wise and visionary individuals concerned about our children and our future. Some, but not all, of their comments are incorporated into the text.

Obviously, there are hundreds of others whose opinions would enhance our thinking. We have sought some of those additional opinions to add even greater validity and to place various issues in a broader context. We have left other opinions and conclusions to be generated through serious discussions of this publication.

Method of Research

To gain insights into how to prepare students for the 21st century, we asked our panel to participate in a somewhat modified Delphi study, a method used to obtain the most reliable consensus from a panel of experts. These experts (our Council of advisers is listed on pages 73-76) were asked repeatedly to answer questions and to comment on other council members' thoughts in three rounds of surveys.

➡ Survey #1 asked our advisers to list answers to various questions about preparing students for the 21st century, based on their personal and professional observations and experiences. These responses were collated by "key word," and issues were identified by the number of times the key word responses were mentioned. Responses were triggered by use of the following queries:

- List what you consider five of the most essential things today's students will need to know to be well-educated for the 21st century.
- List five of the most essential skills today's students will need to have in order to be well-educated for the 21st century.
- List five behaviors that will need to be changed or reinforced in order to prepare students for the 21st century.
- List three changes you believe elementary and secondary schools will need to make to better prepare students for the 21st century.
- State three things parents must do to better prepare children for the 21st century.
- State three things all citizens, including those who have no children in school, must do to ensure that students are prepared for the 21st century.
- State three things state and federal government must do to ensure students are well prepared for the 21st century.
- State three things business/industry/professional leaders could do to help prepare students for the 21st century.
- Do you have other thoughts and suggestions about what we should include in this book?

➡ Survey #2 listed the top responses to each question asked in the first survey. Council members were asked to rank these responses in priority order and to indicate whether they thought each issue had a high, medium, or low impact on preparing students for the 21st century.

➡ Survey #3 detailed the rankings each issue received by both importance and impact. Panel members were then asked to review the data and add any comments that would clarify an item's meaning, influence its importance, or suggest its implications for the future.

The results of these three rounds of surveys are what you have before you — a stimulating discussion starter for schools, school systems, and communities as we prepare our children and youth for challenging lives and what we hope will be bright futures.

COMMON THEMES

Inherent in this probe of some of our nation's prominent thinkers, educators, and futurists is a search for common themes or directions and educational goals for students as they approach adulthood. While debate over the actual purposes of education may rage until the last revolution of our planet, we have assumed that among those goals are citizenship, employability, and personal fulfillment.

During the course of this study, too, several common themes emerged. For example, technology was listed in both the content and the skills sections, as were other items. These common threads emphasize what students need to be successful in the 21st century, and serve as a cue to school leaders that it is no longer sufficient to teach discrete facts by subject area.

Specifically, from the modified Delphi process, six key areas emerged from the results:

1. **Communication.** For the 21st century, communication will be critical. Students must have speaking, listening, and writing skills as well as human relations skills that will enable them to work with others as team members. Students also will be called upon to resolve disagreements through conflict management and negotiation. Parents will be asked to communicate with their children and with their children's teachers and schools. Businesspeople, parents, and other citizens will be asked to get involved — as volunteers, partners, and role models.

2. **Increased support for education.** Schools will need additional support, and funding is a vital part of it. However, other types of support also are needed. Students will be asked to show support for education by respecting their teachers and other educators. Schools will be asked to commit more professional development time for teachers. Parents and other members of the community will be asked to recognize the tangible connection between education and a strong America and to welcome the concept of lifelong learning. Businesses will be asked to share their leadership by contributing resources and getting involved in education. In addition, employers will be called upon to demonstrate the value of education by hiring competent workers and insisting on the importance of graduation requirements and academic performance.

3. **Ethics.** Ethics emerged as a key, overriding issue in many areas of the Delphi study. Parents and businesses were asked to model moral and ethical behavior. Children must learn the importance of being responsible for their own actions and be grounded in sound ethics and self-discipline. Panel members felt that to be successful in the future, students need to value honesty, integrity, and effort. Children and youth must take increased responsibility for their own actions, including setting goals and assessing their own progress. They need to respect others and understand that it is people's differences that make America the land of the free. They must also learn to respect legitimate authority.

4. **Technology.** Students will need to be skilled not only in accessing the vast array of information available through advanced technology, but in processing it as well. Because of the key role of technology in our society, students must know how to use computers and be familiar with various types of technology. To prepare students in this area, schools must incorporate "marketplace" technologies in schools and link with businesses that can share resources, expectations, and vision.

5. **Standards.** The new millennium will bring an increased emphasis on standards and accountability. Schools will be called upon to develop and clarify student goals and standards and periodically assess progress. Both government and citizens not only will assist in developing standards, but help set expectations for student results.

6. **Social and cultural understanding.** Throughout the Delphi study, in nearly every category, the need to understand history, world geography, and foreign languages stood out. The fact that communication and transportation are making our world smaller means we must understand other people and cultures and appreciate diversity. The overall need to prepare students to understand their society and its multiplicity of cultures also was among the most prominent needs expressed.

Times Have Changed:
A Backdrop of Concern for Our Nation's Children

For those growing up in the '40s and '50s, day-to-day life both on and off school campuses was radically different from life in the '90s. You may remember being chided by teachers for chewing gum, talking in class, or failing to line up properly in the lunch room. Back then, for most students, "drugs" were penicillin or aspirin, and "gangs" were close friends who got together after school to play.

Today, students often engage in unhealthy habits including "widespread tobacco and alcohol use, unprotected sex, unsafe driving, staying out overnight without parental permission, and carrying a weapon," according to a 1992 National Center for Health Statistics study of 10,645 children and youth ranging in age from 12 to 21.

By 1995, the Phi Delta Kappa/Gallup Poll on Public Attitudes Toward the Public Schools revealed that 68 percent of parents with children in school had growing concerns about the effects of violence on the nation's schools.

Against this backdrop of social disarray, conditions affecting the nation's children have steadily gotten worse, making education in the classroom even more difficult. In the early 1990s, 25 percent of American children under six lived in poverty, compared to 14.5 percent of Americans of all ages. That fact alone is an indication that we desperately need to care even more for and about our children.

David Orlich, writing in "Social Challenges to America 2000," cites the following facts:

➡ Four in 10 urban school students are absent on a given day.

➡ Of all children born in 1983, 50 percent will live with only one parent at some point before the year 2001.

➡ Children comprise 25 percent of homeless people in America.

"Economic hardship has long stolen childhood from the poor," Lucinda Franks wrote in a *New York Times* article entitled, "Little People." Even children considered from "fortunate" families are affected by vastly changed conditions. Franks argues that middle- and upper-middle income families have "reinvented—or even bypassed—childhood as we knew it." About today's kids, she says, "They are proud, independent, and strong-willed; they are worldly-wise and morally serious. They are a generation that has been raised to challenge and doubt authority, to take little at face value—in short, to enter a world of maturity before they are mature."

A 1995 American Association of School Administrators study on how students have changed since the 1960s revealed the following trends:

➡ The number of "dysfunctional" families has grown.

- High technology has influenced school, work, and home life.

- Children are threatened by crime, violence, ignorance, and poverty.

- Communities are changing and becoming more diverse.

- Mass media grip our children, giving them more knowledge at an earlier age.

- Children shun authority, traditional values, and responsibilities.

- A hurry-up society often lacks a sense of community.

- Changing workplace demands create a need for higher levels of literacy.

- Knowledge about learning styles demands new kinds of education.

- Peers exert a powerful influence on values.

The Challenge to Schools

While these growing challenges may seem overwhelming, the nation's schools are committed to taking students as they are, and to making sure they are well-prepared for life in the 21st century.

Schools and communities need information, expanded thinking, and in-depth discussion as they work, often against great odds, to improve their students' prospects for the future. This work of the Council of 55 is aimed at informing and enriching those discussions.

HOW TO USE THIS BOOK

Here are some steps schools and communities might want to consider in bringing this study to life:

▶ Distribute *Preparing Students for the 21st Century* to school board members, administrators, teachers, and active community leaders, such as parents, business and professional people, local and state government officials, and others.

▶ Share the study with curriculum councils, committees, or task forces for their consideration as they make recommendations or decisions.

▶ Discuss the results of this study with PTA and other parent groups, business and professional leaders, and government officials.

▶ Consider conducting a similar study in your community.

▶ Meet with reporters to share with them the results of this AASA study and what your schools are doing that is similar to or different from recommendations from the Council of 55. If you conduct your own study, show how results in your community compare with the national study.

▶ Carry staff and community newsletter articles about the results of this study and any follow-up study you might conduct.

▶ Use the information gleaned in this study in speeches and various media appearances.

▶ Use this study to focus interest on substantive issues in education and to further educate your community about the needs of schools and how they can help.

CHAPTER 1:

What Students Must Know To Succeed in the 21st Century

What Academic Content Will Students Need to Master To Succeed in the 21st Century?

1. Math, logic, and reasoning skills; functional and operational literacy; and an understanding of statistics.
2. Critical interpersonal skills, including speaking, listening, and the ability to be part of a team.
3. Effective information accessing and processing skills using technology.
4. Writing skills to enable students to communicate effectively.
5. Knowledge of American history and government to function in a democratic society and an understanding of issues surrounding patriotism.
6. Scientific knowledge base, including applied science.
7. An understanding of the history of the world and of world affairs.
8. Multicultural understanding, including insights into diversity and the need for an international perspective.
9. Knowledge of foreign languages
10. Knowledge of world geography.

- Other key content
- An integrated curriculum

In 1908, Harvard President Charles William Eliot recommended that schools tailor their curricula to different students depending on their "evident or probable destinies." Several decades later, former U.S. Secretary of Education William J. Bennett said we must help children "find a better destiny."

Our Council of 55 educators, businesspeople, sociologists, and futurists envisioned that students will need the following academic content, skills, and behaviors to find this "better destiny":

SECTION I:
Academic Content

What will students need to know to be well-educated for the 21st century? According to the Council of 55, here are some essential elements necessary to the content of education:

1. Use of math, logic, and reasoning skills; functional and operational literacy; and an understanding of statistics.

Jan Mokros, writing in *Math Textbooks: Where is Math?*, notes that the term "mathematics" comes from "a family of Greek words denoting to learn or search for meaning." Mokros objects to many math textbooks because "students who use them never have a chance to gather, describe, summarize, and interpret real data for themselves."

"Math must also be viewed as a language and as a way of communicating or making sense of the world," according to Stephanie Pace Marshall, executive direc-

6

tor of the Illinois Mathematics and Science Academy. "Math is a language of relationships, patterns, and connection," she adds. "This is the mathematics we must teach."

The National Council of Teachers of Mathematics has led a pioneering effort to establish standards for the teaching of math. As with any standards, they should guide schools in developing and judging the content, teaching, and evaluation of math curriculum. An understanding of math concepts, computation, and problem solving is essential to a truly literate person.

Math is one way to generate thinking and reasoning skills among students. Performance-based assessments that ask students to reveal how they arrived at answers to math problems can also give students practice in reaching logical conclusions.

As part of the Math Counts program, *USA Today* published a poster showing a front page of the newspaper and highlighting how some knowledge of statistics was necessary to understand nearly every article. Students will need to know not only how to interpret statistics, but also how to determine their authenticity. They also will need to be able to use legitimate statistics to build a case for their ideas. In addition, well-educated students must be able to sort out and evaluate mounds of evidence bombarding them from an expanding number of sources, ranging from textbooks to the Internet.

Learning to reason. Teaching thinking and reasoning skills goes far beyond math. It is a part of every discipline, from writing to studying the causes and the effects of historic events. "Reasoning is not a separate category of learning. It is integral to any lesson, any exercise, any educational experience," says Mary Bicouvaris, the 1989 National Teacher of the Year, who currently is associate professor of education at Christopher Newport University in Newport News, Virginia.

2. Critical interpersonal skills, including speaking, listening, and the ability to be part of a team.

"Interpersonal skills include more than speaking and listening. Students need the ability to work collaboratively with different people," says Anne Campbell. Campbell is a former Nebraska Commissioner of Education and served as a member of the National Commission on Excellence in Education, which developed the 1983 report, "A Nation at Risk."

The ability to work with and communicate effectively with others was an overarching issue in this study. In fact, it placed as an essential part of knowledge, skills, and behaviors.

The Council of 55 made several points about the importance of this critical body of knowledge and cluster of skills:

➡ "Respect for other opinions and perspectives is increasingly vital in a more demographically diverse society," says Michael Usdan, president of the Institute for Educational Leadership.

➥ "More emphasis needs to be placed on achieving these skills through the teaching of core subject areas," adds Chris Pipho, director of state/clearinghouse services for the Education Commission of the States.

The bottom line for some Council members was that interpersonal and communications skills are at the front line of "getting you hired or fired." Others emphasized that the classroom should be a laboratory for collaborative decision making and team building, urging principals and teachers to model the behavior by collaborating. One panelist remarked, "Students will not buy into the 'do as I say, not as I do' syndrome."

3. Effective information accessing and processing skills using technology.

The spotlight of the nation and much of the world is focused on more effectively accessing the plethora of information that is virtually at our fingertips. Concern continues to grow about an expanding gulf that may divide the information rich and the information poor. Education cannot stop with simply helping students learn to access information. Students also will need to understand how to process and use the volumes of often conflicting information that will reach them each and every day. "Everyone says you must be able to read," says Marvin Cetron, president of Forecasting International and a chief advisor for this study. "It's more important for us to understand that we now have videodiscs; we have tools we can use interactively. Now, with technology, you can learn by seeing and doing."

Some students will be expected to create new technologies. Others will be expected to explain technology in plain language. Thus, both technical and communication skills will continue to be valued simultaneously.

"We need more effective training for teachers to emphasize information accessing and processing, plus we need to ensure that all students have access to technology," says Mary Hatwood Futrell, dean of the George Washington University Graduate School of Education and Human Development, and a former president of the National Education Association.

Of course, both the technological tools and the knowledge and skills needed to use them are essential to education for the 21st century. "Education at all levels will require large increases in funding to provide the equipment and training for teachers to meet the demand for technology in the curriculum," according to Jack Dulaney, superintendent of the Monongalia County Schools in West Virginia. "This may require asking more businesses to become involved." Adds Marshall, "We must go beyond information accessing to include information creation and knowledge development."

4. Writing skills to enable students to communicate effectively.

Writing is one of the essential elements of literacy. It is a key to effective communication, and the very act of writing demands thinking and reasoning. Writing helps individuals develop initiative as they sort through ideas, organize thoughts, and draw parallels. It develops courage, since sharing ideas leaves them open to the scrutiny of others. Writing also has been shown to contribute to even better reading skills.

Writes Kathryn Au, an education psychologist with the Kamehameha School in Honolulu, Hawaii, "If we want students to become good readers and writers, we need to involve them in the full processes of reading and writing. We should have them read literature and write for a variety of purposes, just as we want them to do in real life."

The National Council of Teachers of English has done extensive research on effectively teaching students to write. While debate continues over the importance of mechanics vs. free and creative writing, the fact remains that both are important. Ultimately, students need to be able to write to inform, to persuade, to express, and perhaps even to entertain.

Keeping current. We should keep in mind that language itself evolves, and so do writing styles. Members of the Council of 55 suggested continuing in-depth training for teachers, coupled with providing students with sound materials and practical experiences in writing. They also emphasized the need for students to be able to write creatively and scientifically and to be able to use tools such as hardware and software to assist them in writing, editing, and rewriting (often considered among the most important steps in the writing process). (See also page 16 in the skills section of this chapter.)

5. **Knowledge of American history and government to function in a democratic society and an understanding of issues surrounding patriotism.**

"Becoming involved in our representative democracy is critical for our nation's future," said Thomas Shannon, executive director of the National School Boards Association. "When students get involved, theory touches reality," he added.

Indeed, the best way to learn about civics is to become a part of it. Of course, a knowledge of history and government is key to avoiding pitfalls of the past.

Key concepts. During 1995, the Center for Civic Education, working with a number of other groups, released standards focusing on five significant questions:

1) What are civic life, politics, and government?

2) What are the foundations of the American political system?

3) How does the government established by the Constitution embody the purposes, values, and principles of American democracy?

4) What is the relationship of the United States to other nations and to world affairs?

5) What are the roles of the citizen in American democracy?

These questions, plus a framework found in a report on those standards, "We The People...The Citizens and the Constitution," are essential touchstones for developing effective programs to teach students about their government and to guide them in the teaching of history. Of course, state and local history as well as family and recent history are important in connecting with the continuum of social, political, and economic development.

In "Education for Democracy," a joint project of the American Federation of Teachers, the Educational Excellence Network, and Freedom House, three convictions were presented for "schools to purposely impart the ideals of a free society." They are: "First, that democracy is the worthiest form of human government conceived. Second, that we cannot take its survival or its spread—or its perfection in practice—for granted. Third, that democracy's survival depends upon our transmitting to each new generation the political vision of liberty and equality that unites us as Americans."

The National Council for the Social Studies and other subject area organizations have intensified their focus on preparing students to function in a free and democratic society. The issue of patriotism raised several comments among members of the Council of 55. "It is important that students have knowledge about the democratic process and not just blind patriotism," emphasized former superintendent K. Jessie Kobayashi.

Panel members also appealed for integration in the teaching of history, government, geography, and other social sciences to show how they all are related and interconnected.

6. Scientific knowledge base, including applied science.

"One cannot just learn *about* science," says Marshall. "Science is the active engagement with the physical world. It is risk, experimentation, failure, and discovery. It must be *experienced*."

Scientific discovery and the practical and commercial applications of discoveries have brought profound changes to the nation and the world. Most would agree that leadership in science is directly connected to our nation's capacity to maintain a sound economy and may even determine whether the nation or the planet will survive. Therefore, science education, from knowledge about scientific principles, to applied science, to an understanding that, over time, evidence may suggest new theories, is essential.

Science for all. "All of our children and young adults, not just those preparing to be professional scientists, must have an understanding of scientific ways of thinking and science knowledge in order to function in an information age," writes Mary Lewis Sivertsen in *Transforming Ideas for Teaching and Learning Science* , published by the U.S. Department of Education. "Equally important is the ability for all citizens to make good decisions using a basic understanding of the science and technology behind the various social issues affecting their lives."

As superintendent of the Princeton, New Jersey, Public Schools, Paul Houston, currently executive director of the American Association of School

A NATION AT RISK

Perhaps no other clarion call sounded as loudly as a 1983 report from the National Commission on Excellence in Education entitled "A Nation at Risk: The Imperative for Educational Reform." Years later, it was still quoted in arguments over how well education is serving the American public. Despite reform efforts large and small, most people are unclear whether the status of education, as it is described in the report, has fundamentally changed.

The NCEE was appointed in 1981 by former U.S. Secretary of Education T.H. Bell. Similar to previous commissions, it was made up almost entirely of educators and education representatives, including superintendents, teachers, principals, executives of education associations, presidents of universities, and one ex-governor.

Their charge was to:

▶ Assess the quality of teaching and learning in public and private schools, as well as colleges and universities.

▶ Compare American schools with those of other advanced nations.

▶ Study the relationship between college admissions requirements and student achievement in high school.

▶ Identify educational programs that result in notable student success in college.

▶ Assess the degree to which major social and educational changes in the recent past have affected student achievement.

▶ Define problems that must be overcome in order to pursue excellence in education.

The group concluded that American students did not compare favorably with those of other nations; about 13 percent of all 17-year-olds, they said, were functionally illiterate; standardized test scores were down from the 1960s; students did not possess higher order thinking skills; math and science achievement was declining; and business and military leaders were reporting that retraining employees and recruits was costing them millions of dollars.

In brief, the report advocated a "New Basics" emphasis including the following recommendations:

▶ **English.** Among other skills, students should be able to comprehend, interpret, evaluate, and use what they read; they should write well, and know our literary heritage and how it relates to everyday life.

▶ **Math.** Students should be able to apply mathematical principles in everyday situations, and estimate, measure, and test the accuracy of their calculations.

▶ **Science.** Students should understand the social and environmental implications of scientific and technological development, and understand the process of scientific inquiry.

▶ **Social studies.** Students should understand the "broad sweep" of historical and contemporary ideas, understand the fundamentals of our economic and political systems, and grasp the difference between a free and a repressive society.

▶ **Computer science.** Schools should equip students to understand the computer as an information, computation, and communication device.

In all areas, the report called for students to be able to apply their knowledge in day-to-day life.

Administrators, worked with a community planning group that discussed whether technology drives values or vice versa. Their answer was that technology does drive values. (For example, our abilities to extend life through technology and medicine are increasing, which leads to questions about how we define "life," the morality of euthanasia, and more.) Therefore, as science and technology are applied in real-world situations, ethics and values must be developed to guide their use.

Start early. In her report, Sivertsen notes that science has remained a relatively low priority in elementary schools, yet the elementary grades are a critical time for capturing children's interest. "If students are not encouraged to follow their curiosity about the natural world in the primary grades, waiting to teach science on a regular basis in grade four may be too late. Data show that many children tend to lose interest in science at about the fourth grade," she says.

Percy Bates, director of Programs for Educational Opportunity at the University of Michigan School of Education, says that "for too long the field of science has seemed to be reserved only for the bright, the smart, the elite in our schools." In an Equity Coalition article, "Science Education and Equity," Bates cites evidence from the National Center for Educational Statistics, dated June 1992, showing that "Boys and girls are virtually even in math and science achievement in the third and seventh grades. However, by the 11th grade, boys achieve at a much higher level than girls." He encourages the "removal of all barriers in the field of science. Evidence shows that not only gender, but race, ethnicity, and socioeconomic class (SES) are acting as gatekeepers to becoming a scientist."

Superintendent Jack Dulaney sums it up this way: "Science concepts and theory must be a part of the curriculum for all students. Therefore, the application of learning becomes as important as the theory."

Recent work of the National Science Teachers Association and organizations representing various disciplines within science education, the American Academy for the Advancement of Science, and the National Science Foundation, has resulted in ideas and information for improving science education at all levels.

7. An understanding of history of the world and world affairs.

As much as some people would like to think of their nation as an island detached from the rest of the world, it is simply no longer possible to maintain that separation. Political, technological, sociological, economic, and environmental issues jump both natural and political borders. They affect us all. Therefore, students need to understand world history and world affairs.

An understanding of world history and world affairs could help today's students avoid future Holocausts or explore how various nations might become allies in conquering disease or reaching into inner, outer, and cyberspace.

Tom Maes, superintendent of the Adams County School District #1 in suburban Denver, Colorado, believes, "Like languages, the lack of world history has serious implications for world markets." Adds NSBA's Shannon:

Patriotism, founded on pride in our national, political culture, traditions, and institutions is clearly important. But this does not mean that knowledge, respect, and appreciation of other cultures and nationalities should be sloughed. We are in a mutually interdependent world and must get along—but not at the price of surrendering our own values.

Students need to be grounded in the cultures of other peoples, if only to understand them and to maintain peace in an interdependent world.

8. Multicultural understanding, including insights into diversity and the need for an international perspective.

The world has become more interrelated as satellites, cyberspace, and jet travel bring people and nations closer together. Communication transcends political boundaries. Our nation, too, has become more cosmopolitan as new waves of immigrants come to America. In fact, except for Native Americans, the United States is a land of immigrants. All are seeking common as well as divergent purposes in a free and democratic society. Now, more than ever, an understanding of diversity is key. In the future it will only become more important.

The ability to work in collaboration with different people is critical, says Richard Warner, principal of Fargo South High School in North Dakota. "Different people means not only color, but gender, nationality, religion, and political persuasion," he adds. "The basic need is for understanding our dependency on each other," says California superintendent K. Jesse Kobayashi.

Other members of the panel also called for not only the teaching of multicultural understanding but also the modeling of it in every school and community.

Properly managed, diversity can enrich. Not properly managed, it can divide. The key is education.

9. Knowledge of foreign languages.

"How can we provide a sound education and compete in world markets without learning foreign languages?" asks Maes. For that matter, how can we make ourselves understood if we aren't able to communicate in languages of the world marketplace? How can we be sure we aren't being taken advantage of because we don't understand the conversations taking place around us? How can we fully enjoy the history and culture of other nations or of the immigrants who come to this country without an understanding of other languages? These are questions demanding our attention as we approach the 21st century.

OTHER KEY CONTENT

KNOWLEDGE OF ARTS AND HUMANITIES

While the arts and humanities were recognized by the Council of 55 as crucial, they did not rank as high as math, science, or communications skills. However, members of the panel saw these key aspects of education as cross-cutting.

Judith Billings, state superintendent of public instruction for the state of Washington, says, "These areas are not only important, but essential for the development of a well-educated, responsible citizen." Moreover, Floretta McKenzie, president of the McKenzie Group and advisor for this book, says, "I'm concerned that we're not emphasizing aesthetics enough. The arts seem to provide the color for one's life, while everything else might be in black and white."

How is it possible to study history without examining the arts? How is it possible to appreciate music, writing, visual images, dance, design, architecture, even the handiwork of nature without an appreciation for the arts? The arts provide a basic means of communication. They help students develop their creative talents, and can aid schools in teaching other subjects. The arts open a window on human civilization, help students develop self-discipline, prepare students for their adult lives, and enhance students' artistic judgment. The arts have practical, professional, and emotional value.

Standards for arts education, developed by the American Council for the Arts in 1992, guide schools planning for the 21st century. For example, schools no longer teach only applied arts, but also an appreciation of art history. Also, instructors teach real-world applications, such as typography and other graphic principles in art classes, in addition to drawing, painting, and pottery.

In 1994 President Bill Clinton remarked at an Art-I Conference, "As we become increasingly diverse...the arts can help us understand each other, honor our differences, and appreciate the experiences and beliefs we share as Americans." McKenzie adds, "We need to develop Renaissance people who have a high appreciation of the arts, while also having high-level skills to do whatever necessary to earn money."

The late President John Kennedy said, "I am certain that after the dust of centuries has passed over our cities, we too will be remembered not for victories or defeats in battle or politics, but for our contribution to the human spirit."

A GROUNDING IN ETHICS

"Ethics are essential," says Stephanie Pace Marshall, executive director of the Illinois Mathematics and Science Academy. "Values and morality can be taught only when we decide to agree on who we are, what are the underpinnings of our civilization, whose works and thoughts influenced the founders of our country, and what common values we respect," former teacher of the year Mary Bicouvaris emphasized.

Ethics represented another cross-cutting issue for the Council of 55. Concern about ethics, morality, and values was reflected in every category—knowledge, skills, and behaviors.

Superintendent Jack Dulaney says, "The school environment must be a place where values, morality, ethics, honesty, and responsibility are not just taught in isolation or as an adjunct to other content that consumes instructional time. These values must be the example, the rule, the way that the business of educating or teaching is conducted at all levels.

"We need whole people; we need thinking people; we need people with solid ethics," adds McKenzie.

The stories are legion. Businesspeople from other countries come to the United States and speak our language. Americans go to other countries and need interpreters. As businesses become increasingly multinational and as nations pool resources to collaborate on global issues, such as the environment, the lack of ability to communicate in other languages becomes an even more costly barrier.

10. Knowledge of world geography.

Similarly, a lack of knowledge about geography will be a barrier to understanding our shrinking universe. Anthony R. DeSouza, in "Time for Geography: The New National Standards," writes:

> By the year 2000, planet Earth will be more crowded, the physical environment more threatened, natural resources more depleted, the global economy more competitive, world events more interconnected, human life more complex, and the need for people to have a solid grasp of geography even more essential.

He adds, "By learning geography thoroughly, students come to understand the connections and relationships among themselves and people, places, cultures, and economies across the world."

An Integrated Curriculum

While the Council of 55 identified fairly specific disciplines or bodies of knowledge that will be required for students to thrive in the 21st century, as mentioned earlier, members of the Council also made clear that the curriculum should be integrated across disciplines. "Perhaps history, government, geography, and other social sciences need to be integrated," Dulaney suggests. "This will show students the connections and interrelationships."

"It seems that with the emphasis on an integrated curriculum across disciplines as well as the need for students to learn to work collaboratively, this will lead to a new curriculum of the 21st century," says J.C. Sparkman, former executive vice president of Tele-Communications, Inc. (TCI) of Denver.

Moving in the direction of a more integrated curriculum will take some rethinking of critical linkages, however, according to panel members. Michael Usdan, president of the Institute for Educational Leadership, questions, "How do we move colleges to deviate from traditional teaching of academic disciplines, since higher education often helps determine the secondary school curriculum?"

Staff development for teaching an integrated curriculum was also an issue with the Council. "Does a district offer content staff development?" asks Chris Pipho, of the Education Commission of the States. "Are principals equipped to offer teachers help in curriculum areas, or is it available from another source?"

What Skills Will Students Need for the 21st Century?

1. Oral and written communication skills.

2. Critical thinking, reasoning, and problem-solving skills.

3. Self-discipline.

4. Skill in the use of computers and other technologies.

5. Job success skills.

6. Adaptability and flexibility.

7. Conflict resolution and negotiation skills.

8. Being able to conduct research and interpret and apply data.

9. Knowledge of other languages—being multilingual.

10. Comprehensive reading and understanding skills.

SECTION 2:

Essential Skills

What are the most essential skills students will need to be well-educated for the 21st century? According to the Council of 55, to be prepared for the future students will need:

1. Oral and written communication skills.

Clear communication—both oral and written—is critical to success, said former superintendent K. Jessie Kobayashi. Other panelists agreed.

One reason is that teamwork and other new models in the workplace will require communication ranging from face-to-face to messages exchanged through sometimes faceless electronic systems. In the marketplace of ideas, the person who communicates clearly also is the person who is seen as thinking clearly. Oral and written communication are not only job-securing—but job-holding skills.

George Bernard Shaw observed that "The greatest problem of communication is the illusion that it has been accomplished." Therefore, students need to understand the communication process. They need to understand the concepts of sender and receiver, to be able to trace how communication might have broken down, and to understand the art of follow-through. As well, they will need a grounding in nonverbal communication, since simple gestures can either reinforce or erase a message.

As cyberspace grows, cable systems expand, digital communication provides nearly instant access, and satellites connect us with other parts of the nation and world, the resulting information overload will increase the pressure on individuals to be able to think, reason, and communicate effectively.

(See also the academic content section, page 6.)

2. Critical thinking, reasoning, and problem-solving skills.

In 1961, the Educational Policies Commission announced that "the purpose which runs through...all educational purposes...is the development of the ability to think." Indeed, an urgent call has been raised nationwide and even worldwide about the need for students to make even better judgments, to think and reason more effectively, and to solve problems.

In the early 1970s, education researchers observed that teachers allowed an average of two seconds for students to respond to direct questions. Simply increasing the wait to three to five seconds brought more thoughtful responses.

Information is the new source of America's power—its new capital. Obviously, with information as a major commodity, students must be prepared to sort it out, think about it, combine it, and consider its benefits and consequences.

"When hiring people, employers want critical thinking and problem-solving skills," according to Stephen Kleinsmith, director of secondary education for the Millard Public Schools in Omaha, Nebraska.

However, simply solving problems may not be enough. "It is essential to teach students problem finding and resolving skills, says Stephanie Pace Marshall of the Illinois Mathematics and Science Academy. Marshall also notes that students should not become too attached to their conclusions. "In the real world, problems are usually solved for a time until new data are secured, and then the solution changes. Students must know that problems are never solved in real life as easily as they are on television," she says.

While critical thinking is important, so is creative thinking, or thinking "outside the box." While inductive and deductive reasoning skills provide a logical framework for reaching conclusions, occasionally students will need to think laterally and rely on flashes of insight that go far beyond the traditional reasoning processes. Students must also learn to apply certain technologies in developing solutions to problems and to override those solutions when they fall outside an ethical framework.

3. **Being self-disciplined, acting responsibly, applying ethical principles, and setting and assessing goals.**

Concern about ethical behavior permeated this study. Today's children and youth are bombarded with examples of unethical behavior from television, radio, and newspapers, and the bad example set by many adults.

Yet, to survive and prosper in the 21st century, students will need self-discipline, which entails an ethical code and the ability to set and assess progress toward their own goals. According to one panel member, schools must provide opportunities for students to assume a role in goal-setting, planning, and assessment of progress toward meeting goals so that they will begin to understand the concept of responsibility. Adds Christopher Cross, president of the Council for Basic Education, "Thinking skills are essential. Perhaps more ought to be taught."

"The ability to anticipate future consequences of actions is vital, but we must also add a sense of feeling of individual responsibility for personal actions," emphasizes Thomas Shannon, executive director of the National School Boards Association. (See also the academic content section, page 6, and the behaviors section, page 20.)

4. **Skill in the use of computers and other technologies.**

While the Council of 55 recognized the importance of computers and other technologies as tools in delivering academic content, members of the Council also pointed out the need for students to develop skills in operating and making the most of these largely electronic systems.

"These skills are essential," says Anne Campbell, former Nebraska Education Commissioner. "Computers and all forms of technology must be fully incorporated into the curriculum—NOW," she added. "We can't wait until the year 2000," agrees Jack Dulaney, superintendent of Monongalia County Schools in Morgantown, West Virginia.

In an interview with *Technos* magazine, Linda Darling-Hammond, professor of education at Teachers College, Columbia University, and co-director of the National Center for Restructuring Education, Schools, and Teaching, addresses the role of technology in schools. Technology has several roles to play, she notes. The redesign of schools is in part intended to help us focus on active learning—doing research, accessing information, using resources to answer questions and solve problems. Computer technology and databases can be enormously helpful in allowing students to look for information in a variety of ways. For example, teachers on-line can share ideas, debate issues, display authentic assessments to one another, and more.

5. Job success skills, including good interpersonal and human relations skills and the ability to work as part of a team.

Getting and keeping a job in the 21st century will very likely require good interpersonal and human relations skills. Even with the increase in home-based businesses, virtual and satellite offices, interpersonal skills will divide the workers from the achievers. Most still will need to communicate with others, whether it be face-to-face, electronically, or otherwise. Indeed, the "depersonalization" of some forms of communication probably will make those who can overcome this hurdle even more valuable. "School-to-work transition programs will have to enhance these skills," says Pipho.

"Interpersonal and human relations skills will be needed in the future," says Dulaney. "Technology will not replace the personal involvement required among workers and managers as the technological age evolves."

Whether the skills are applied in person or through other forms of communication, collaboration will be essential. Marshall suggests schools organize "collaborative learning environments" to give students more experience in dealing with others.

In a 1992 *Wall Street Journal* article, "Academe Gets Lessons from Big Business," John Kelsch, director of quality at Xerox, called for students who can work in groups. "We want to hire students who are better prepared for our world. We want them to be customer-oriented, to work in team environments, and we want them to understand work as a result of processes," Kelsch said.

6. Adaptability and flexibility.

In a fast-changing world, students will need a catalog of skills broad and deep enough to allow them to adapt, and attitudes that encourage flexibility.

"The ability to get along will be as critical as mastering subject matter content," says Mary Hatwood Futrell, of the George Washington University.

"People skills remain important in all fields and endeavors," according to Michael Usdan, president of the Institute for Educational Leadership in Washington, D.C. "Students must learn to be flexible as both leaders and followers," Usdan said.

7. Conflict resolution and negotiation skills.

When people know how to work out their differences they often experience breakthroughs in mindsets, and can resolve problems more easily. These skills may even save lives.

"People are becoming more vocal, more challenging," says Cross. In today's increasingly violent society, many feel their lives are at stake when conflict escalates and those involved lack the skills to resolve it. Without these skills, fists and weapons replace dialogue.

Within families and organizations, students who will live their lives in the 21st century also will need skills in negotiation. While these skills have most often been seen as the purview of labor negotiators or diplomats, they will become increasingly essential. Finding "win-win" solutions will be part of seeking common ground and dealing with our differences.

8. Being able to conduct research and interpret and apply data.

To thrive in the 21st century, students will need to be able to conduct various types of research and to interpret and apply data. Their library and media skills need to be finely honed, and their reasoning abilities must always be on alert.

Schools may wish to bring people into the classroom who can demonstrate how research and gathering, interpreting, and applying data are important to them in their jobs or professions, says Dulaney. Real-life examples often enliven student interest. Of course, schools will need to provide ready access to the world of information through print, electronic, and face-to-face channels, and to provide students with an opportunity to test their theories, based on what they find.

"Students must have ready access to information in abundance. This shifts the focus from teaching to learning, and learning is a process," concludes Marshall.

9. Knowledge of other languages—being multilingual.

Once again, knowledge of other languages emerges as paramount. "We must encourage more students to become bilingual, to learn another language, and to learn about different cultures," says Futrell.

Colorado superintendent Maes agrees. "We can't even get along with our neighbors unless we know who they are and can communicate with them."

Skills in effectively communicating in more than one language are increasingly important as our marketplace becomes more international. The benefits and consequences bear on such important issues as economic competitiveness and world peace, as well as knowing and appreciating our neighbors. (See also the academic content section, page 6.)

10. Comprehensive reading and understanding skills.

In 1647, leaders of the Massachusetts Bay Colony mandated public reading instruction. Today, reading continues to be central to education and one of the primary requirements for literacy.

While the merits of reading words and reading for comprehension are a subject of constant discussion, and while phonics vs. whole language instruction is frequently debated, the fact remains—our children must read well if they hope to do well in the 21st century.

Coupled with reading are listening, speaking, writing, and thinking skills. Most would agree that reading is a cross-cutting skill that is basic to all other areas of the curriculum.

SECTION 3:

Behaviors

According to J.C. Sparkman, former executive vice president of Tele-Communications, Inc., "We must address the social issues raised if schools are going to have a chance in the future."

According to the Council of 55, the following are among the behaviors that students will need to exhibit if they are to be successful in the 21st century.

1. Understanding and practicing honesty, integrity, and the "golden rule."

Treating others as we would like to be treated, personal and organizational integrity, and basic honesty came up time after time, in nearly every section of this study. In some cases, the term "ethics" was used, in other cases "character." Perhaps driven by violence in the streets, ethics transgressions in the government and elsewhere, and because people find themselves too often the victims of unethical behavior, this item became a cornerstone of the study for members of the Council of 55.

As one panel member noted, a problem is that we don't always model the best behavior for students, or provide them with good examples in school curricula. Some suggested that conflict resolution teams, collaborative learning, mentorships, the study of classic stories, character education, and role models in the community would help to reinforce ethical behavior.

(See also pages 6 and 16 in the content and skills sections.)

2. Respect for the value of effort, understanding the work ethic and need for individual contributions, and self-discipline.

Council member Adam Urbanski, president of the Rochester Teachers Association in New York, notes that students who will be successful in the 21st century will know "the importance of making an effort, or trying to do well."

Once again, discipline was a recurring theme, and again, self-discipline was emphasized. After all, it will be self-disciplined young people who will ensure that this country remains not only economically competitive, but free and democratic. Without self-discipline, talents are squandered.

Adds Bicouvaris, "Schools need to place a stronger emphasis on discipline as a positive form of behavior." The same is true with the application of talents and abilities in the workplace and community. An attitude that work is good, and that individual as well as team efforts are useful and even exhilarating, can lead to greater productivity in society, better communities, and vastly increased personal satisfaction.

Lessons learned off campus. While some of these behaviors are influenced at school through career education, participation in school activities such as volunteering, athletics, academic clubs, and others, and through character education, they also are reinforced or undermined in the home and in the community at large. For example, when parents encourage their children to do their homework and when they show them the benefits of setting, pursuing, and achieving goals, they are helping them develop a good work ethic and a sense of self-discipline.

Baltimore Orioles shortstop Cal Ripken, who surpassed Lou Gehrig's record when he completed 2,131 consecutive games on Sept. 6, 1995, brought to light many stories of people who have reported to work every day for years on end because they feel it is the right thing to do. Perhaps one of the reasons the media hooked into the Ripken story so eagerly was because that attitude is seen as unusual. It is not surprising, then, that panel members remarked on the necessity of instilling in children the value of effort and personal responsibility.

3. **Understanding and respect for those not like you—an appreciation of diversity.**

The concept of appreciating diversity cuts across all areas of this study, including the areas of knowledge and skill. "This is a critical behavior to live in a

THE COMMITTEE OF 10

At the turn of the century in 1892, the National Education Association assembled a "Committee of 10" distinguished educators whose charge was to study ways of developing good citizenship in the schools. Chaired by Harvard President Charles Eliot, the committee recommended an eight-year intensive course in history spanning the fifth through 12th grades.

Basically, the Committee of 10 asserted that "When historical studies are taught in conjunction with literature, geography, and foreign languages they serve to broaden and cultivate the mind...they counteract a narrow and provincial spirit...they prepare the pupil ...for enlightened and intellectual enjoyment...and they assist him to exercise a salutary influence upon the affairs of his country."

diverse United States," says Arnold Fege, director of governmental relations for the National PTA. In a pluralistic society, understanding and respecting others of various races, ethnic groups, religious beliefs, genders, and so on, represents the fulfillment of the nation's motto, "E Pluribus Unum," which means "Of the many...one." Some have expressed alarm that our "pluribus" has increased but that our "unum" has decreased, which creates an even greater demand for reinforcing this principle.

Some panel members made clear that people need to earn respect, however. Former National Teacher of the Year Mary Bicouvaris puts it this way: "Respect must be given and also earned. Just because others are not like us, they do not automatically deserve our respect should they behave in a way that does not earn our respect."

Jack Dulaney says, "Respect for others must become a community-wide value. Then it may be modeled in the schools."

4. Capability to work with others as a team member.

According to an Aug. 13, 1995, article in *The Washington Post*, "As many as half of the nation's workers will be organized in teams by the year 2000. Generally, teams combine workers from a variety of areas into a single unit to achieve a common goal. Employees oversee projects, devise their own strategies, and even manage operations."

The need to be able to work with others was reinforced in every area of this study. So important was this behavior to members of the Council of 55 that they highlighted it under knowledge and skills, as well as behaviors.

People, organizations, parts of organizations, and even nations, are interdependent. The ability of people to combine their knowledge and talents to achieve an even higher purpose is synergistic and will be essential to life in the 21st century.

"Opportunities must be offered to enable students to work and learn in a team-like environment," says Dulaney. (See also the academic content section on page 6).

5. Taking increased responsibility for one's own actions.

Our nation has long focused on teaching people about their rights in a free and democratic society, and those rights are important. However, we will only be able to maintain those rights so long as we exert a sense of responsibility toward society. Whether an effort or a society is successful or unsuccessful will depend largely on what individuals are willing to put into it.

In many cases, people write off their responsibility by blaming others for failures. In other cases, people declare themselves victims when they have allowed themselves to become victimized.

An even better society and an even better life for every person in it will depend on individual and group responsibility. Some of these behaviors can be reinforced through educators and others in the community modeling how they want others to act. Some can be taught by bringing to life standards for civics education, released during the mid-1990s. (See page 9.)

6. Respect for others and for authority.

This item also is cross-cutting, bearing on the golden rule, respect for the value of effort, multicultural understanding, conflict resolution, and the ability to work constructively as a member of a team. Respecting others is basic to a civil society.

In the 1995 Phi Delta Kappa/Gallup Poll on Public Attitudes Toward the Public Schools, the public remained concerned about violence in our society and how it affects the nation's and their local schools. In that poll, parents cited fighting, violence, gangs, and a lack of discipline and control as prominent problems. Violence against others is, to an extent, the ultimate breakdown of respect and civility. That is perhaps a reason why respect for authority surfaced in more than one part of this study.

Concern was expressed by panel members that those in authority need to earn their respect by being *respectable*, since many young people are skeptical of behaviors exhibited by some individuals, organizations, and governments. Blind respect for authority has led to some of the most outrageous crimes committed against humankind.

"Authority must earn respect," cautions the NSBA's Thomas Shannon. "This is a subtle nuance for most young people. There has to be a balance in teaching this. Otherwise, if

THE PAIDEIA PROPOSAL

Mortimer J. Adler, a noted philosopher and professor at the University of North Carolina at Chapel Hill, spearheaded a group of distinguished educators and others including these individuals, who held the following positions at the time: Ernest Boyer, president of the Carnegie Foundation for the Advancement of Teaching; Alonzo Crim, superintendent of the Atlanta, Georgia, public schools; Clifton Fadiman, author and critic; Jacques Barzun, literary adviser of Charles Scribner and Sons and former provost of Columbia University; Ruth Love, general superintendent of schools, Chicago Board of Education; and Theodore Sizer, chairman, A Study of High Schools, and former headmaster, Phillips Academy-Andover, among others. The work of this Paideia group, compiled in a 1982 book called *The Paideia Proposal*, castigated the practice of tracking students into ability groups and outlined a one-track system with high standards for all students. In brief, they believed schools should provide all students with avenues for the following:

- **Personal growth or self-improvement** (mental, moral, and spiritual). "Every child should be able to look forward not only to growing up, but also to continued growth in all human dimensions throughout life."

- **An adequate preparation for discharging the duties and responsibilities of citizenship.** Without this goal in sight, schooling produces "an ignorant electorate and amounts to a travesty of democratic institutions and processes. Schools must cultivate the civic virtues and teach the framework of our government and its principles."

- **Learning the basics.** This item refers to those skills that are common to all work in a society, so that adults can earn a living.

individual views of authority's legitimacy or credibility are allowed to control, it's nothing but an invitation to anarchy."

7. Commitment to family life, personal life, and community.

"Without these, what is there?" asks Council member Maes. Shannon adds, "A sense of community to reinforce family is critical in the formation of character, which, as Teddy Roosevelt used to say, is the foundation for all values."

Schools can help students build these behaviors through social studies, civics education, school-to-work and community involvement programs, and other activities. However, schools can't do it alone. As with other behaviors, they must be reinforced by family and community.

8. Pride in United States citizenship and knowledge of individual responsibilities in a democracy.

Ideally, students should feel empowered and motivated to constantly improve their communities, state, and nation. Rather than simply being critical, students who will live most of their lives in the 21st century will need to take such pride in the potential of democracy and such responsibility as citizens that they will shape society to become even more civil.

In 1995, the Royal Bank of Canada published an article titled, "The Duty of Civility," in its *Royal Bank Newsletter*. The article stated:

Civility means a great deal more than just being nice to one another; it is the lubricant that keeps a society running smoothly....Civility calls upon us to make an effort to see the other person's point of view, and to try to resolve differences democratically. It allows us to engage in dialogues with those whose ideas we oppose in a non-aggressive fashion. This leads to attempts to reconcile disagreements by seeking and moving toward common ground."

The national standards for civics education, developed by the Center for Civic Education and others, provide guidance for helping students develop behaviors that support and build democracy and reinforce civility. Superintendent Jack Dulaney notes, "All students must develop the skills necessary to participate in the democratic process. This goes beyond a history or civics class. Instead, real-life opportunities to observe and participate in the democratic process must be provided."

9. Willingness to civilly resolve disagreements.

Each day, America discovers anew the cost of conflict. History records the high price of war and unresolved issues. The daily newspaper brings word of another domestic or street fight that has led to destruction, injury, and even death. Somehow, according to the Council of 55, students must have a willingness and ability to civilly resolve disagreements, a theme that runs throughout this study. (See also the skills section, page 16.)

What can schools do to build and reinforce behaviors that lead to the peaceful resolution of conflict? Some schools are offering conflict resolution and

The Seven Cardinal Principles

In 1918 the National Education Association's Commission on the Reorganization of Secondary Education (CRSE) wrote a now famous report, "The Seven Cardinal Principles," that outlined by what criteria secondary school offerings would be judged. Like the Committee of 10, members of the Commission represented only the education field, and included both secondary and higher education experts. Copies of this report were circulated by the U.S. Bureau of Education. The principles were these:

1. Health
2. Command of fundamental processes
3. Worthy home-membership
4. Vocation
5. Citizenship
6. Worthy use of leisure
7. Ethical character.

It is worth noting that, even then, members of the educational community and their constituents believed strongly in the notion of tying schooling to the social agenda. In fact, number 2, "command of fundamental processes," which might characterize a more traditional view of the purpose of education, was not listed in the original report and was a late add-on.

The report stated that education should be driven "by the needs of the society to be served, the character of the individuals to be educated, and the knowledge of educational theory and practice available," as well as the real-life skills adults need to succeed. The latter issue did little to further the rights of girls and women, however. The Commission urged that the status of homemaking in curriculum be boosted to give girls the skills they would need as adults.

peer mediation programs for students, faculty, administration, and parents. Some are helping students better understand each other through multicultural education.

In one Fairfax County, Virginia, elementary school, students learn about concepts such as responsibility and choices, and ways to respond to conflict. Students learn about conflict resolution from a "peace teacher" and the school counselor, and nominate each other for good behavior recognition.

10. Recognition and respect for educators.

Educators in this country don't get much recognition and respect. Other countries have much more respect for their educators. Those are statements heard over and over again in the United States.

Unless educators are held in high regard, the schools of our nation will have an increasingly hard time attracting the brightest and best into education careers.

"If recognition and respect for teachers and public educators is *not* considered essential for the 21st century, where will our teachers come from?" asks Stephanie Pace Marshall. "We must create those conditions that attract commitment and talent to teaching," she concludes.

Floretta McKenzie adds, "A respect for learning, excellent study skills, and parents who support and believe in schools can make a difference. In some Asian cultures, there is a greater respect for learning and for teachers, and more Asian students apply themselves than some of our students in America." She adds, "I would suspect that if we could change the way we treat teachers, have respect for education, and mobilize communities to realize how important education is, we would see a difference in student performance."

11. Being excited about life and setting goals for lifelong learning.

"Students need to focus on what they'd like to do in life," says Mary Hatwood Futrell. Members of the Council of 55 suggest that society and various institutions in society, such as the family, religious groups, business and professional organizations, and schools need to help young people find purpose in life. As for schools, one panel member noted "Faculty and principals must involve students, parents, and the community in a goal-setting process."

In the 1994 update of his work, *What Schools Are For*, author John Goodlad notes that schools can help foster lifelong learning in students:

> The American public school is responsible not only for educating citizens to develop and maintain a democratic society, but also for engendering in individuals the desire to continue their education throughout their lives....The school can help individual students to clarify their aspirations, develop a step-by-step process for the attainment of those aspirations, monitor their progress, and try to understand and alleviate the problems they encounter.

What's in it for me?

Sadly, some believe that good behavior for its own sake is a thing of the past. Futurist David Pearce Snyder, a member of the Council of 55, observed:

> Since surveys show that one-half to two-thirds of all high school students today believe that the future will be worse than the present, it will be difficult for educators to convince young people to practice such socially constructive behaviors as the work ethic, respect for authority, the golden rule, tolerance, etc., without some demonstrable evidence that such behaviors are producing visible economic rewards and benefits which apply to them.

In the following chapter, we'll explore what schools can do to help their children become even better prepared for life in the 21st century.

CHAPTER 2

What Schools Can Do To Prepare Students for the 21st Century

What Changes Schools Can Make To Better Prepare Students for the 21st Century

1. Incorporate "marketplace" technology in learning and as part of graduation requirements, and ensure that new and emerging technologies are incorporated into the school program.
2. Respect all students' abilities to learn by promoting "active" versus passive learning.
3. Commit more time for professional development for teachers and administrators.
4. Develop world-class standards, redefine the basics, and clarify what is expected of students.
5. Provide more time for students and teachers to work on "real world" projects.
6. Increase parental and community involvement in schools.
7. Strengthen the authority and control of schools and teachers.
8. Create new systems that strengthen the connections among the school, the home, and the workplace to complement school learning.
9. Reflect an international perspective in the curriculum.

"Education is learning what you didn't even know you didn't know"

— Ralph Waldo Emerson

What follows are the most essential changes needed in elementary and secondary schools to prepare students for the 21st century, according to the Council of 55.

Lee Hager, assistant superintendent of curriculum and instruction for Flagstaff Unified School District in Arizona, cautions, "We must understand that one solution doesn't fit every school district's situation. We have a diverse set of school systems in the nation, and we mustn't be tempted to apply the same rules to all." With this in mind, the Council of 55 came up with these suggestions:

1. Incorporate "marketplace" technology in learning and as part of graduation requirements, and ensure that new and emerging technologies are incorporated into the school program.

To cultural anthropologist Jennifer James, "The society that succeeds will be the one that uses information most effectively." For one thing, the world of work is changing drastically, and students must be prepared to enter a very different work life. "We are seeing more 'portfolio professionals' who can work from home and work anywhere in the world. We are starting to live in technological cottages," notes James.

The Michigan State Board of Education's Model Core Curriculum of 1991 emphasized the importance of technology:

The technologically literate person is one who understands the role and impact of technology upon society, accepts the responsibilities associated with living in the technologically oriented information age...and uses technology as a tool for obtaining, organizing, (and) manipulating information and for communication and creative expression.

Working with information must be second nature to Michigan's students. Graduates must know how to sort fact from fiction, how to decide when a given fact is relevant, and why one technique works instead of another, making it easier for them to create new processes that stand a good chance of solving a unique and significant problem.

Endless possibilities. Technology has changed the way the world does business, opening up global economic competition and offering nearly limitless opportunities. While students in the 1970s might have learned about the human heart using a plastic model, students in the 1990s dissect a human heart with the help of computer-aided design. In addition to looking up information in the school library's encyclopedias, students of the '90s connect with interactive information available on CD-ROM or on the Internet. "If there's one thing schools and students have over their parents it's the utilization of advanced, current, technologies," says Larry Decker, parental involvement

MULTIPLE INTELLIGENCES

Howard Gardner, professor of education at Harvard University and co-director of "Project Zero," hypothesizes that human beings are capable of developing at least seven different "intelligences":

▶ **Linguistic.** Sensitivity to language, meanings, and the relationships among words. Characteristic of writers, journalists, and public relations professionals.

▶ **Logical.** Mathematical intelligence constitutes abstract thought, precision, counting, organization, logical structure. Characteristic of mathematicians, scientists, engineers, police officers, lawyers, and accountants.

▶ **Musical.** The sensitivity to pitch, rhythm, timbre, the emotional power and complex organization of music. Characteristic of performers, composers, conductors, recording engineers, and instrument makers.

▶ **Spatial.** Keen observation, visual thinking, mental images, metaphor, a sense of the whole. Characteristic of architects, painters, sculptors, navigators, chess players, and physicists.

▶ **Bodily/kinesthetic.** Control of one's body and of objects, timing, trained responses that function like reflexes. Characteristic of dancers, athletes, actors, inventors, and surgeons.

▶ **Interpersonal.** Sensitivity to others, ability to read the intentions and desires of others and potentially to influence them. Characteristic of politicians, teachers, religious leaders, counselors, and sales people.

▶ **Intrapersonal.** Self-knowledge, sensitivity to one's own values, purpose, feelings, a developed sense of self. Characteristic of novelists, counselors, philosophers, and gurus.

expert and C.S. Mott Professor in the department of education at Florida Atlantic University.

Noted futurist Marvin Cetron, president of Forecasting International, predicts that new technologies will greatly improve education and training. In his article, "An American Renaissance In The Year 2000," Cetron says that "Personal computers with ultra-high-resolution screens, 3-D graphics, high-level interactivity, artificial intelligence, and virtual reality will enhance gaming and simulations used in education and training." He also predicts that education will become more individualized, as interactive computer/videodisc systems and other new media permit students to learn according to their specific needs and abilities.

Of course, depending on how they are used, these technologies can contribute to even better education or offer serious distractions. With computer networks virtually exploding, schools will be faced with issues ranging from sorting out the multitude of information available on worldwide networks to dealing with concerns about student access to cyberporn.

The Council of 55 recommended ways to make optimal use of current technology in the schools. "Incorporating technology in the schools will also require computer literacy for *all* teachers and administrators," says Jennifer James. Making the business community an involved and active participant as schools incorporate technology was mentioned by several of our experts, as well. (See also Chapter 1, pgs. 6 and 16 for cross-cutting information.)

2. Respect all students' abilities to learn by promoting "active" versus passive learning.

Students do best when they are learning actively, rather than simply listening to lectures. Some active learning practices include hands-on projects, Socratic questioning, cooperative learning, manipulatives, field trips, and experiments.

"Learning is no longer a separate activity that occurs either before one enters the workplace or in remote classroom settings," says author Suoshana Zuboff (*In the Age of the Smart Machine*, 1988). She adds, "The behaviors that define learning and the behaviors that define being productive are one and the same. Learning is not something that requires time out from being engaged in productive activity; learning is the heart of productive activity. To put it simply, learning is the new form of labor."

"Our schools are changing," explains the Oregon Department of Education in its publication, *Oregon Schools for the 21st Century*. "First- and second-graders study climate and geology by transforming their classroom into a glacier-covered mountain. Eighth-graders topple balsa wood towers to study earthquakes. High schoolers use computers to link teachers with students at three locations and learn about the local economy by growing plants for nearby businesses."

Anne Campbell, former Nebraska Commissioner of Education and a member of the National Commission on Excellence in Education, feels that students need to experience both active and passive learning. "How are students going to be dedicated to thinking and acting on their own? Learning takes place singly as well as together," she cautions.

In an *Education Digest* article, "Will 21st Century Schools Really Be Different," Linda Darling-Hammond, of the Teachers College at Columbia University, states that one area of school reform is creating learner-centered schools that focus on learners' needs rather than standardized procedures. "This means allowing teachers and others to organize to work with students in ways that address the whole child and look at learning holistically."

Equity is an issue in learning, too. Schools today are moving toward more inclusive models that try to allow all children access to excellent, active learning activities. Special education students are being mainstreamed, and educators are rethinking tracking programs that sort and separate children. Mary Bicouvaris, associate professor of education at the Christopher Newport University who was the 1989 Teacher of the Year, notes that "Students are accountable for their achievement as long as they are afforded the instruction that is available to all."

3. Commit greater time for professional development for teachers and administrators.

"We must educate men and women in considerable numbers to become engines of change," says George Lodge in *Work in the 21st Century: An Anthology of Writings on the Changing World of Work*.

Floretta McKenzie, president of the McKenzie Group and former superintendent of the Washington, D.C., public schools, adds, "We need to invest in our teachers. Teachers need more professional development and more experiences in the application of their subject to the real world."

"Successful classroom innovations, such as team teaching and incorporating an integrated curriculum, also require substantial training, as does teamwork, the most productive organizational innovation of the 1980s and 1990s," says one Council member.

Professional development, although often required in corporate America, too often gets short shrift in education. Darling-Hammond agrees that "most schools are not structured to allow teachers to learn from one another or to share what they know." She sees one path to transforming teaching into a more respected profession as "evaluation that enables teachers to engage in peer coaching and mentoring programs." Many teachers are not ready for the shift to more active learning without staff development and appropriate materials and equipment. "Adult-to-adult time in schools is always overlooked as being important," says Council member Richard Warner, principal of Fargo South High School in North Dakota. He adds that while professionals within the schools are a great resource, they seldom get called on to share with their fellow educators.

"Professional development is crucial," says Campbell. "Change in classrooms is a slow process of perseverance and acceptance," she adds. "This shouldn't be accomplished at the expense of instructional time," cautions Council member Stephen Kleinsmith, director of secondary education for Millard Public Schools in Omaha, Nebraska.

4. Develop world-class standards, redefine the basics, and clarify what is expected of students.

"We must know where we are going if we want to know when we get there," says Tom Maes, superintendent of Adams County School District #1 in suburban Denver, Colorado, to capture the essence of the standards debate. How will schools be accountable for student achievement? How will achievement be measured? These are simple questions, yet they have sparked controversy within many school communities.

In 1995, the American Federation of Teachers launched a grassroots campaign calling for schools to emphasize discipline and higher academic standards. In announcing the campaign, AFT President Albert Shanker, a member of the Council of 55, said, "Other education reforms may work. High standards for conduct and achievement do work...and nothing else can work without them." Shanker noted that the effort was consistent with findings of both the 1995 Gallup Poll on Public Attitudes Toward the Public Schools and a survey conducted by the Public Agenda Foundation.

"The public and state legislatures will increasingly demand an assessment of student achievements and hold schools accountable," emphasizes Cetron. He also predicts that more states will adopt the national education goals as part of an effort to assess their schools' performance. As of mid-1995, all but a few states had become part of the federal-state partnership Goals 2000 program, which is intended to set voluntary national standards for curriculum content and student performance. (For more information on standards, see Chapter 4.)

Heavy obligations. "We need to clarify our standards in education," says Kleinsmith. "But," he cautions, "will we ever have a 'world-class' educational system as long as we are also 'recreational' institutions and 'social' agencies? A lot of our effort and dollars go into both recreational and social obligations along with our educational responsibility for academics." To help alleviate the strain on schools, Council member Christopher Cross, president of the Council for Basic Education, believes that "schools need to cooperate with social service agencies to bring them into schools." However, Mary Jarvis, principal of Smoky Hill High School in Denver's suburban Cherry Creek School District and another member of the Council of 55, adds "If schools become more like social service agencies, who pays?"

Fair or not... Certainly schools are expected to provide more and deal with more social concerns than ever before. To illustrate the changing face of America, Paul Houston, executive director of the American Association of School Administrators, has created a satirical "Leave it to Beaver" scenario for his speech, "Winning the Race with the Clock, or Postcards from the Edge." He refers to television characters such as Wally, Ward, and June. In the television show "Leave it to Beaver," which aired in the late 1950s, Houston said, "Ward went to work, June kept the house, and their sons—Wally and the Beav—went to school. Today's version would find that Ward would be in prison, June would be a welfare mother, Wally would be on drugs, pal Eddie Haskell would be a Blood or a Crip, and the Beaver would definitely be at risk."

"Schools and colleges must reconsider the need for new models. Recertification standards and regional accrediting standards are responsibile for some of our current situation," says Chris Pipho, division director of clearinghouse/state relations for the Education Commission of the States. "Much will be done in this arena, especially in school finance and accountability programs," he adds.

> ## Maine's Common Core Outcomes
>
> ▶ **The human record.** Focuses on student understanding of history and the constructs of human thought and creativity as they have evolved over time.
>
> ▶ **Reasoning and problem solving.** Focuses on students' ability to use knowledge and to reflect on their own process of learning.
>
> ▶ **Communication.** Develops students' ability to use a variety of media.
>
> ▶ **Personal and global stewardship.** Focuses on the development of responsible citizens and personal well-being.
>
> *Adapted from Maine's Common Core of Learning.*

"We should emphasize the need for setting a vision for each school and the school system," adds Arizona assistant superintendent Lee Hager. In speaking of state plans and vision statements, Walt Warfield, executive director of the Illinois Association of School Administrators, notes, "Clearly the best of plans are going to be achieved when there's support behind them," including moral, political, and technical, as well as financial, support.

5. Provide more time for students and teachers to work on "real world" projects.

Cognitive theorists, including Howard Gardner of Harvard University, argue that educators err when they assume students "know" things because they are able to parrot back facts or theories or apply their knowledge to routine problems. Seldom does such knowing include an understanding that allows students to apply knowledge in new settings.

More and more, students are demanding that what they learn actually connects to the real world. Growing numbers of students, too, look for some connection between what they are learning and later economic benefit. If it doesn't benefit them, or isn't usable, they are likely to lose interest.

Many students have heard promises of better jobs and a better life if they study hard and do well in school, only to see their friends who did just that end up unemployed.

"Schools need to change," says Floretta McKenzie. "The connection to the real world is critical. For many students, particularly poor students, they don't see the connection between what they learn in school and what they will do when they leave school."

Students may also need entrepreneurial skills as traditional employer-employee relationships wane.

The message is clear: Schools need to make what they teach more relevant to the real world, while businesses and others who hire graduates need to pay more attention to what students have studied and how they accommodate this knowledge in the work setting. Schools can do this by encouraging teachers to use examples from life in problem solving, asking students to relate themes from literature to current events or apply scientific principles to solving ecological problems, and teaching practical applications of math, such as balancing a checkbook or figuring out percentages, among other methods.

6. Increase parental and community involvement in schools.

Panel members agreed that parental involvement in schools is important. "We must establish parent advisory councils that have a purpose other than simply forming a group that is in name only," emphasizes Council member Jack Dulaney, superintendent of Monongalia County Schools in Morgantown, West Virginia. "This means schools must hold community forums and conduct surveys to secure input from parents," he adds.

"Researchers tell us that teachers are not trained to deal with parents, and are

An Educational Vision

This vision of education for Illinois schoolchildren was developed by citizens of the state through a process supported by Gov. Jim Edgar, the Illinois State Board of Education, the Illinois Business Roundtable, and school leaders.

World-Class Education for the 21st Century:
The Challenge and the Vision

As we approach the 21st century, there is broad-based agreement that the education we provide for our children will determine America's future role in the community of nations, the character of our society, and the quality of our individual lives. Thus, education has become the most important responsibility of our nation and our state, with an imperative for bold new directions and renewed commitments.

To meet the global challenges this responsibility presents, the state of Illinois will provide the leadership necessary to guarantee access to a system of high-quality public education. This system will develop in all students the knowledge, understanding, skills and attitudes that will enable all residents to lead productive and fulfilling lives in a complex and changing society. All students will be provided appropriate and adequate opportunities to learn to:

▸ Communicate with words, numbers, visual images, symbols, and sounds.

▸ Think analytically and creatively, and be able to solve problems to meet personal, social, and academic needs.

▸ Develop physical and emotional well-being.

▸ Contribute as citizens in local, state, national, and global communities.

▸ Work independently and cooperatively in groups.

▸ Understand and appreciate the diversity of our world and the interdependence of its peoples.

▸ Contribute to the economic well-being of society; and

▸ Continue to learn throughout their lives.

largely unprepared to work with parents in a genuinely collaborative way," says futurist David Pearce Snyder, also a member of the Council of 55. "As with other genuine innovations, the creation of productive collaborations between parents and teachers, and between administrators and community institutions, will require substantial new initiatives and aggressive commitments by school leaders, plus a significant investment in training for educators, parents, and community members," Snyder adds. (For more information on parent involvement, please see Chapter 2.)

7. Strengthen the authority and control of schools and teachers.

Some see local school councils and other forms of site-based management and decision making as a way to more deeply involve staff and community in decisions, to increase a sense of overall ownership, and to get everyone working in a common direction. Others see them as attempts to get around a bureaucratic system.

"The adoption of site-based management is the single most productive reform that school districts can adopt," says futurist Snyder. "Experience has shown that delegating to individual schools the authority over their own resources and curriculum is the most effective way to foster the rapid adoption of significant innovations."

To be sure such activities help instead of hinder progress, school boards and administrators need to make sure training and information are offered and that expectations are clear. "Without such training," Snyder adds, "it is clear that most teachers and local administrators are simply unable to make purposeful uses of their newly-delegated authority."

The work of a local school council, for example, should be focused on what is best for all students and not on narrow interests. Right up front, the roles and responsibilities of these groups and their reporting relationships should be clear.

8. Create new systems that strengthen the connections among the school, the home, and the workplace to complement school learning.

Cetron believes that improved pedagogy, which he defines as the science of learning, will revolutionize education. "Individuals will learn more on their own, so the 'places' of learning will be more dispersed, and the age at which things are learned will depend on individual ability, not tradition," he says. In addition, Cetron believes that lifelong education and training services will be in demand. "Schools will educate and train both children and adults around the clock: The academic day will stretch to seven hours for children; adults will work a 32-hour week and prepare for their next job in the remaining time."

Council member J.C. Sparkman sees schools eventually extending their resources to the home electronically. Other experts predict that community agencies in the future will work even more collaboratively with schools to address the social, economic, and psychological factors that affect the stability of the home and,therefore, student success. For example, many schools and districts employ family resource coordinators to visit homes. Other schools house community health or computer centers that serve the needs of students and parents. These are just a few ways schools can reach out to serve their communities, and ultimately, their children.

9. Reflect an international perspective in the curriculum.

"Students need to be aware of and understand the world in which they live and work," says Mary Hatwood Futrell, dean of the George Washington University Graduate School of Education and Human Development. With the increased interdependence of nations and people, American students need to look beyond their nation's borders and learn to appreciate the similarities and differences in people and cultures that make the United States an economic and political role model for other countries.

We also need to make clear that students must be able to compete for jobs in the international marketplace, which also will entail a better understanding of other people and their cultures, as well as communication skills of an international scope. (The international perspective is discussed in Chapter 1, What Students Need to Know for the 21st Century.)

A Common Core of Learning: Experts on What Schools Need To Teach

ERNEST BOYER

In his book, *High School*, Boyer recommends that for those living in the United States, the mastery of English is crucial. Some of his recommendations include teaching students to read and comprehend the main ideas in a written work; learning correct sentence structures, verb forms, punctuation, word choice, and spelling; and monitoring each child's proficiency in oral and written English. He calls letting students with limited English proficiency pass from one grade to another without special help "a cruel hoax."

> "Language defines our humanity. It is the means by which we cope socially and succeed educationally. The advent of the information age raises to new levels of urgency the need for all students to be effective in their use of the written and the spoken word. The mastery of English is the first and most essential goal of education."
>
> —Ernest L. Boyer, *High School: A Report on Secondary Education in America.* The Carnegie Foundation for the Advancement of Teaching, New York: Harper and Row, 1983.

Spoken language should be emphasized: Boyer urges a return to what was once called the teaching of rhetoric. He proposes a speech course that would include group discussion, formal debate, public speaking, and reading aloud.

Conversely, listening skills also are important to life, he says. Students should be taught to "evaluate what they hear, to understand how ideas can be clarified or distorted, to explore how the accuracy and reliability of an oral message can be tested."

Boyer also recommends a common core of learning that spans literature, the arts, foreign languages, history, civics, science, mathematics, technology, and health. In terms of implementing this, Boyer proposes restructuring curriculum to increase the number of required courses from about one-half to two-thirds of graduation credits. This curriculum would emphasize foreign languages, technology, civics, non-Western studies, the arts, health, and the importance of work. Finally, Boyer's vision includes a senior project to help students move "from courses to coherence."

Boyer advocates that schools teach "global thinking," so that students do not stay painfully ignorant of a world constantly shrinking because of technological advances:

The globe has changed. If the high schools are to educate students about their world, new curriculum priorities must be set. If a school district is incapable of naming the things it wants high school graduates to know, if a community is unable to define the culture it wants high school graduates to inherit, if education cannot help students see relationships beyond their own personal ones, then each new generation will remain dangerously ignorant, and its capacity to live confidently and responsibly will be diminished.

THE EFFECTIVE SCHOOLS MOVEMENT

In 1966, University of Chicago sociologist James S. Coleman spurred debate when he published a report entitled "Equality of Educational Opportunity," which held that children's general social context was more of a factor than education in determining whether or not they achieved. Fueled by their objections to this theory, a group of researchers began studying child development in mostly poor and minority urban districts. One of these researchers, James Comer, a Yale psychiatrist and director of the university's Child Study Center, believed that schools could educate these children better if they helped alleviate some of the psychological and social problems limiting children's development. Comer piloted a program in two New Haven public elementary schools, and noticed improvements in learning and parental participation within three years.

Another researcher, George Weber, found through his study of effective urban schools that they all shared these characteristics: strong leadership; high expectations for all students; an orderly atmosphere; and an emphasis on pupil acquisition of reading skills, reinforced through frequent monitoring and evaluation.

Ronald Edmonds, who served at different times with both the Michigan Department of Education and Harvard University, took the research a step further. He worked with University of Michigan educators Lawrence Lezotte and Wilbur Brookover to devise the following "correlates" of effective schools: [sic]

1. Strong administrative leadership.

2. A climate of expectation in which no children are permitted to fall below minimum but efficacious levels of achievement.

3. The school's atmosphere is orderly but not rigid, quiet without being oppressive, and generally conducive to the business at hand.

4. Effective schools get that way partly by making it clear that pupil acquisition of basic skills takes precedence over all other school activities.

5. The principal and teachers must be constantly aware of pupil progress toward the instructional objectives through frequent testing.

JAMES MADISON HIGH SCHOOL

William J. Bennett, U.S. Secretary of Education from 1985 to 1988, published two books detailing what he believed to be the "shared body of knowledge, the common language of ideas, and the moral and intellectual discipline that Americans want their children to possess" (*James Madison Elementary School*, U.S. Department of Education, 1988, p. 1.). In *James Madison High School*, Bennett stressed that this model, while based on experiences with real schools, was meant to be a goal and an ideal, not a strict curriculum to be imposed across the board. Implicit in his argument is high standards and expectations for all students; he criticized those who believed schools should tailor lessons based on any subjective notions of who can and can't learn.

Specifically, *James Madison High School* describes a curriculum of vigorous classical studies including four years of English, three years each of math and science, two years each of foreign languages and physical education, a half-year each of art and music, and some electives.

Bennett advocated that English, social studies, and physical education/health courses be taught in a set sequence. In math, science, foreign language, and fine arts, the sequence would be more flexible to accommodate student interests, needs, and abilities.

Like Boyer, Bennett's vision included an emphasis on the acquisition of foreign languages, probably in anticipation of increased diversity. His concept of a course in the principles of technology also is noteworthy. Unlike Boyer, Bennett made no mention of preparing for the world of work.

CULTURAL LITERACY

In his controversial work, *Cultural Literacy: What Every American Needs To Know*, E.D. Hirsch, Jr. makes a case for a "national vocabulary" that serves as the underpinning of knowledge to be gained in school. Rather than a national core curriculum, Hirsch advocates cultural literacy, which he defines as "the network of information that all competent readers possess....Cultural literacy lies above the everyday levels of knowledge that everyone possesses and below the expert level known only to specialists. It is the middle ground of cultural knowledge that children need to learn in school."

Hirsch's famous lists of examples in literature, science, math, language, history, social studies, and other fields include thousands of citations of concepts, facts, definitions, works of art and literature, dates, and other categories that he says educated individuals should at least find familiar. For example, the appendix in *Cultural Literacy* lists the following dates: 1066, 1492, 1776, 1861-1865, 1914-1918, and 1939-1945; and these ten terms as the first of many under the letter "A": abbreviation, abolitionism, abominable snowman, abortion, Abraham and Isaac, Absence makes the heart grow fonder, absenteeism, absolute monarchy, and absolute zero.

THE PUBLIC SPEAKS

A 1995 report by the Public Agenda Foundation confirms many of the findings of the study conducted for this book, including the importance of basic skills, self-discipline, and technological know-how.

The following table lists those qualities various constituents thought were necessary for schools to teach students:

Percentage Saying "Absolutely Essential"	GENERAL PUBLIC	PARENTS	TEACHERS	LEADERS
Basic reading, writing and math skills	92%	91%	98%	99%
Good work habits such as being responsible, on time, and disciplined	83%	79%	92%	88%
Computer skills and media technology	80%	78%	88%	75%
The value of hard work	78%	77%	84%	70%
Values such as honesty and tolerance of others	74%	71%	80%	76%
Habits of good citizenship such as voting and caring about the nation	66%	64%	78%	58%
How to deal with social problems like drugs and family breakdown	64%	63%	65%	39%
American history and American geography	63%	61%	83%	61%
Biology, chemistry and physics	59%	56%	65%	43%
Practical job skills for office or industry	57%	55%	57%	33%
Curiosity and a love of learning	57%	61%	69%	61%
Advanced mathematics such as calculus	37%	38%	22%	29%
The history and geography of such places as Europe or Asia	35%	35%	48%	29%
Classic works from such writers as Shakespeare and Plato	23%	21%	33%	21%
Sports and athletics	23%	22%	19%	7%
Modern American writers such as Steinbeck and Hemingway	22%	21%	29%	20%

Source: "Assignment Incomplete: The Unfinished Business of Education Reform." The Public Agenda, 1995.

Hirsch believes that our complex contemporary society depends on the cooperation of many people from different specialties, residing in different places. "Where communication fails, so do the undertakings. The function of national literacy is to foster effective nationwide communications," he says.

Hirsch concludes that while teaching methods and textbooks may vary, an agreed-upon, explicit national vocabulary should in time come to be regarded as the basis of a literate education.

Summary

"Schools must go back to the 'basics' if students are to be prepared for the 21st century," states Stephanie Pace Marshall, executive director of the Illinois Mathematics and Science Academy. She adds that the "basics" are the principles of learning, the relationships between teachers and learners, the fundamentals of establishing a learning environment, and the principles of empowerment.

Cautions Arnold Fege, director of governmental relations for the National PTA, "Piecemeal reform without comprehensive change will be inconsequential in preparing kids for the 21st century. These changes must be results-driven and practical, research-based and substantial."

Now that we've discussed how schools may need to change to better prepare students for the 21st century, let's see how parents can support our children's future.

THE NATIONAL EDUCATION COMMISSION ON TIME AND LEARNING

One of the most sweeping changes in elementary and secondary schools is the use of time. "Educators and the community must be willing to restructure the use of time," says Jack Dulaney, superintendent of Monongalia County Schools in Morgantown, West Virginia. In its report "Prisoners of Time," The National Education Commission on Time and Learning suggested that United States schools should double the time students spend studying academics and expand school hours if they want to offer extracurricular activities. The report noted that an American student spends an average of five and one-half hours in six class periods each school day, but that half that time is devoted to non-academic classes and electives.

The NECTL recommends school districts:

1. Reinvent schools around learning, not time. This means changing the focus from "How much time is enough?" to "What are we trying to accomplish?"
2. Use students' time in new and better ways. Education must be redesigned so that time becomes a factor supporting learning, not a boundary marking its limits.
3. Provide additional academic time by reclaiming the school day for academic instruction. Students must receive at least 5.5 hours of core academic instructional time daily.
4. Keep schools open longer to meet the needs of children and communities.
5. Give teachers the time they need. Teachers must be provided with the professional time and opportunities they need to do their jobs.
6. Invest in technology. Schools must seize on the promise of new technologies to increase productivity, enhance student achievement, and expand learning time.
7. Develop local action plans to transform schools.
8. Share the responsibility. All people, including parents, community members, and government must work together to transform learning in America.

Source: "Prisoners of Time," Report of the National Education Commission on Time and Learning, April 1994.

CHAPTER 3

Parents Hold the Future in Their Hands

What Parents Can Do To Prepare Students for the 21st century

1. Work cooperatively with teachers and the school. Visit and communicate with the school.
2. Support education and schools. Take an active interest in children's school work.
3. Provide a rich, stable home learning environment.
4. Model moral/ethical behavior and decision making.
5. Enhance children's self-esteem through attention and care.
6. Model and value the concept of lifelong learning.
7. Read to and with children.
8. Spend more quality time with children.
9. Monitor homework completion and provide guidance toward goals.
10. Use the best of TV, then turn the rest off. Foster media skills.

"The American family is the rock on which a solid education can and must be built."

—Richard Riley, U.S. Secretary of Education

A parent is a child's first teacher, serving as a model for behavior and providing the guidance and support that build a child's self-esteem and enhances learning.

Though schools have taken on more responsibility for preparing students for their futures, they obviously can't do it alone—nor would parents want them to. Experts surveyed for this publication, and for numerous other studies, say that parental involvement and support are vital to a child's education. With children spending only 9 percent of their time in school between birth and age 18, the home environment is considered crucial to a child's learning.

In looking toward the future, what can parents do even better to prepare their children for the 21st century? Here are 10 suggestions posed by our Council of 55:

1. Work cooperatively with teachers and the school. Visit and communicate with the school.

According to a 1993 study by the National Center for Education Statistics, one of every four public school teachers cited a lack of parent involvement as a serious problem in their schools. And parent involvement tends to taper off as children get older: Secondary school teachers were more likely than elementary school teachers to report lack of parent involvement as a serious problem in their school, according to the report.

When parents work closely with a child's teacher and school, the student is the winner, though all benefit. Depending on their level of involvement, parents gain self-confidence in parenting, an understanding of their home as a learning environment, an understanding of school programs and services, an increased comfort in communicating with the school, and input into policies that affect their children's education. Students gain respect for their parents, receive the message that school is important, and experience a higher level of confidence in doing their schoolwork. Teachers and school systems gain a respect and appreciation of a parent's time, a common base of knowledge for communicating about a student's strengths and weaknesses, and a feeling of parental support for programs.

According to researchers Paul Barton and Richard Coley in *America's Smallest School: The Family*, a 1992 study conducted for the Policy Information Center of the Educational Testing Service, student achievement is directly related to how much time parents talk to their children about school and whether they take an active role in school matters.

Education and parent involvement researchers Anne Henderson, Carl Marburger, and Theodora Ooms, of the now dissolved National Committee for Citizens in Education, outline five roles parents typically play in their children's education:

➡ **Parents as partners.** At this basic level, parents follow their legal and moral obligations to enroll children in school, make sure they attend, are dressed properly, and enter ready to learn. For their part, schools abide by parents' rights, including access to students' records, due process in discipline, and a say in special education decisions.

➡ **Parents as collaborators and problem solvers.** In this role, parents supplement what students learn in school by encouraging and rewarding achievements, providing enrichment activities, enforcing policies about bedtime and homework, and helping schools solve a child's problems as they arise.

WHAT CAN PARENTS DO WITH THEIR CHILDREN?

A PTA/World Book telephone survey asked 830 parents what they thought were essential or highly desirable activities to do with their children:

▶ Talking to their kids about what they do in school (98 percent).

▶ Listening to and talking with their children, paying attention to their questions and feelings, and staying informed about their school work (98 percent).

▶ Showing pride in their child's academic performance (97 percent).

▶ Encouraging their children to go on to higher education (92 percent).

Source: National School Public Relations Association, *Network*, June 1994, p. 5.

➡ **Parents as audience.** Parents attend events at school and stay informed on their child's school life.

→ **Parents as supporters.** This role calls for more time and effort on the part of parents. They may serve as tutors; volunteers, either in their own child's class or elsewhere; school librarians; attendance-call officers; or chaperons for various functions. They work closely with their parent-teacher group and may belong to a parent support network.

→ **Parents as advisers and co-decision makers.** This is the highest level of involvement. Parents may belong to the school board, a local school council, or a site-based decision-making group.

The roles usually build on one another, so that parents involved to the point of serving as advisers and decision makers most likely fulfill the other roles, as well.

While time constraints, language or cultural barriers, or negative past experiences keep some parents from becoming involved with their children's education, parents should know that study after study confirms parental involvement is one of the most important factors influencing student achievement.

2. **Support education and schools. Take an active interest in children's school work.**

Most Americans say they support education and schools—at least their local schools, according to a 1994 study conducted for AASA by Mellman-Lazarus-Lake and the Phi Delta Kappa/Gallup Poll of the Public's Attitudes Toward the Public Schools. Every year the Phi Delta Kappa poll has been given since the 1970s, three-quarters of respondents said they would give local schools a grade of "C" or above; 40 percent would give local schools an "A" or a "B." However, when viewed nationally schools typically fare worse: When asked to grade the public schools as a whole only 20 percent of the 1995 national total would give them an "A" or "B," with only 18 percent of public school parents giving this response. The 1995 poll was the first to probe this disparity. The most frequently cited reasons were that local schools are perceived as placing more emphasis on academic achievement, and having less crime, violence, and racial incidents.

A parent's attitude toward education and school can have a profound impact on student achievement. For example, when parents ask about and check students' school work, when they discuss their children's likes and dislikes, strengths and weaknesses, and otherwise show they care about school, they send a very basic but powerful message: School is important. It is valued.

Larry Decker, Charles Stewart Mott Professor at Florida Atlantic University's College of Education and author of AASA's book, *Getting Parents Involved in Their Children's Education*, says that, at a minimum, children whose parents care about school get encouragement. They get to school on time—they stay in school. In caring families children go to school prepared, with the proper amount of sleep and food. "And when you come home there's an interest," Decker adds. "How did you do, etc."

In the 1987 work, *The Evidence Continues to Grow: Parental Involvement Improves Student Achievement*, author Anne Henderson examined more than 50 studies of parent involvement to form this conclusion:

> Children whose parents help them at home and stay in touch with the school score higher than children of similar aptitude and family background whose parents are not involved. Schools where children are failing improve dramatically when parents are called in to help.

However, schools face the reality of parents working long hours just to make ends meet and finding scant time for their children. That's a direct reflection of changes in society, according to J.C. Sparkman, former executive vice president of Tele-Communications, Inc. "It is apparent from the changing demographics of society that we shouldn't expect parents to supply the same type of support that may have been the case in the past without resources or assistance," Sparkman observes.

3. Provide a rich, stable home learning environment.

Parents can make their homes rich with learning opportunities for children in many ways. For instance, studies have shown that the more reading materials parents provide, the better readers children will be. The local library can supply a constant source of free reading materials. Also, parents can set a good example by reading often themselves. One byproduct of a family that reads is that the TV is on less frequently, which may also improve student achievement.

Children can learn a lot from the daily newspaper. Parents can feature a "person of the week" or "event of the week" to spur discussions, for example.

Decorating a child's room with posters of world maps, a chart of the elements, exotic animals, or letters and numbers for young children provides visual stimulation and a fun learning environment, as well. Children also benefit from colors and shapes they can manipulate, nutritious food, and ways to keep physically fit, such as basketball or other physical activity.

Stability is important for children, as well. Studies indicate that students living with both parents have higher proficiency in school, even controlling for other factors. This isn't always possible, of course. What is important is that a child is loved, nurtured, and given a stable, supportive, and safe home. Children thrive on routines. Parents should try to keep children on a fairly regular schedule for meals, play, and work time. Parents provide stability also by setting limits for their children, such as a ceiling on hours worked outside the home, and a set time to do homework and chores.

Support from the community. "School and community support are vital if we are to link with the home," says Arnold Fege, director of governmental relations of the National PTA. "For many parents, a rich and stable learning environment will also be dependent on a supportive and caring community."

4. Model moral/ethical behavior and decision making.

The Council of 55, in nearly every category of our study, emphasized ethics, coupled with the importance of parents as role models for their children. Parents can model moral and ethical behavior, build self-discipline and self-reliance, pass down values, and help children learn to make responsible decisions in many ways. For example, they can:

➡ **Talk about values with children.** If parents believe it's important to help others, respect the elderly, spend time with family, or treat others politely, they should pass this on to their children.

➡ **Think about the message you send with your actions.** When parents say they value honesty but cheat on their taxes, or condemn racism but tell racist jokes, the message sent by the action is clearer than the words.

➡ **Support your child's values.** For example, many children today are concerned about the environment or the homeless. Parents can support such positive values by helping them with recycling, attending an "earth day" celebration, working in a soup kitchen, or other activity.

➡ **Teach responsible decision making.** Parents might ask their children to think about the consequences of their actions and discuss options. The best way to learn sound decision making is to practice it.

"There are not any big secrets" to passing on basic underlying values to children, Decker notes. Rather, children receiving the proper support from home "do not live in families riddled with hate, crime, and detrimental values such as drugs, racism, and violence."

5. Enhance children's self-esteem through attention and care.

What is self-esteem? "It's having the confidence to believe in myself," says one high school student. Positive self-esteem can help children understand and appreciate themselves with self-confidence, self-respect, and a sense of responsibility. Having high self-esteem also helps children—especially teens—resist negative peer pressure. This is important, because by high school, 58 percent of students say they would first turn to a friend their age for advice. In elementary school, only 23 percent would consult with a friend first, according to Robert Coles '1989 "Girl Scouts Survey on the Beliefs and Moral Values of America's Children."

Tom Barrett, an adolescent and family therapist, says that children with low self-esteem feel disconnected from their families and community. They have an "external locus of control," Barrett says, which means "how they feel about themselves depends on everything and everybody outside of themselves." He adds: "Young people who are externally controlled often gravitate toward other kids who have the qualities they'd like to have, then they take on the identity of the group. This is the way kids get started in gangs, sometimes."

Life lessons. As children and youth become even more enamored with media and their peers, and as their parents spend less time in conversation with them, the result often is an overdependence on peers—those with little life experience. To be truly prepared for the 21st century, students also must be able to learn lessons from those who have had broader experiences in life.

Parents play an instrumental role in their child's self-esteem, or how their child feels about himself or herself. Children who have high self-esteem generally have parents who make them feel loved and valued, praising their successes without berating their failures. Parents who emphasize a child's mistakes or who constantly criticize his or her efforts will contribute to that child's low self-esteem. "Self-esteem is the result of success no less than a cause of it," cautions Adam Urbanski, president of the Rochester Teachers Association. He refers to Phil Schlechty, president of the Center for Leadership in School Reform in Louisville, Kentucky, who believes we should invent tasks at which students can succeed without lowering standards in the process.

6. Model and value the concept of lifelong learning.

"Parents must foster lifelong learning. They must encourage inquiry, questioning, and experimentation," says Stephanie Pace Marshall, executive director of the Illinois Mathematics and Science Academy. Lifelong learning is the idea that each person is constantly learning and growing. How can parents foster this love of learning?

Parents can send a message that people never stop learning by continuing to take classes in adulthood. They can support education, verbally and through their actions. Reading at home for pleasure is another way to keep learning. Other ways include taking weekly trips to the library and making sure each child has a library card. When parents don't know the answer to a child's question, it is OK to say, "I don't know—let's go look it up." That way both the parent and child learn something, and the parent is sending a message to the child that learning never stops.

Also, teaching a child to ask good questions is a good place for parents and schools to start. Anyone who is constructively curious will always be well educated.

7. Read to and with children.

According to a 1994 study by the U.S. Department of Education, the single most important activity for children's eventual success is having someone read aloud to them. The study was based on three decades of research on family involvement, and was part of the Department's National Coalition for Parent Involvement in Education, of which AASA is a member. Indeed, reading aloud is one of the most important regular activities a parent or sibling can do that will help students achieve later in life.

In this age of video games, VCRs, and highly structured schedules with little free time, children don't seem to have much quiet time to read or be read to.

In fact, a 1994 study by the National Center for Educational Statistics found that as a child ages he or she is less likely to read during leisure time: While 56 percent of ninth-graders reported reading on a daily basis, only 27 percent of 17-year-olds said they read for fun daily.

By reading aloud, parents introduce children to literature. They model the importance of reading throughout life. Books help improve a student's vocabulary and familiarity with history, other countries, and lives not his or her own. According to researchers Barton and Coley, the more types of reading materials there are in the home, the higher students' reading proficiency.

Reading to and with children can be a community effort as well. In 1995, U.S. Secretary of Education Richard Riley announced his National Read*Write*Now initiative, in which he encouraged communities to team children with reading partners — parents, recreation leaders, senior citizens, teachers, librarians, and older students — to read with children at least twice a week. Under this program, children are challenged to read 20 minutes each day, five days a week, alone or with a partner. At the time this book was published, 125,000 volunteers had agreed to partner with 425,000 children.

8. Spend more quality time with children.

Council member Paula Short of the Department of Educational Administration at The Penn State University College of Education, says that while quality time is a critical issue, the realities of what families face today may work against it. In fact, the American family has undergone drastic changes during the last 50 years. In 1955, 60 percent of American households had a working father, housewife mother, and two children. The percentage of this "typical American family" dropped to 11 percent by 1980 and 6 percent by 1992, according to demographer Harold Hodgkinson.

This is not meant to imply that women or men should be faulted for working. All have the right to fulfill themselves through careers, not to mention that in today's society most women and men must work out of economic necessity.

But what does this mean for "quality time"? Marilyn Colter, a single mother whose daughter recently graduated magna cum laude, says "I am fortunate to have a college degree and professional job. But after working 10 hours at the office with more work to be completed at home in addition to cooking, cleaning, washing, ironing and worrying about money, the 'quality time' I have with my child is consumed with guilt at not being able to do more, give more, provide more."

Even in two-parent households with both the mother and father working, families spend less time together. A study by the National Family Institute found that the average parent spends 14.5 minutes a day communicating with each child. Of that time, 12.5 minutes are devoted to parental criticism or correction.

One way to make the most of time spent with children is to plan activities the whole family can enjoy, which will stimulate the child's interest, imagination, and self-image. Some examples include taking up a family hobby, such as boating or camping; volunteering together at church or in a retirement or nursing home; or, learning something new together. A quiet evening at home after a leisurely family meal may be the best quality time for many in today's overscheduled world.

9. Monitor homework completion and provide guidance toward goals.

If parents show interest in their child's learning, then the child is more likely to develop a good attitude toward learning that will lead to academic success. At the very minimum, parents can help children by making homework a priority and providing a quiet place where children can study.

AASA's booklet *Brush Up Your Study Skills* recommends parents help children find their best study time, stress a regular time for study, work quietly while a child studies, and praise a child's efforts. Parents should also keep reference books and other materials such as newspapers around the house that reinforce learning.

Parents also can teach students a helpful study method called SQ3R (survey, question, read, restate, review). Briefly, this is a consecutive five-step process. First, students skim the material, then answer the "who," "what," "where," "why" questions. They then read the assignment, followed by restating the main points, and a final review.

Anne Campbell, former Nebraska Commissioner of Education and

TV TIPS

Cable in the Classroom suggests using these tips when watching television with children:

▶ **Use TV to capture your children's curiosity.** Encourage them to go to the library to learn about issues or ideas raised by programs they like. When sensitive topics are raised on TV, seize the opportunity to open a discussion.

▶ **Read more about it.** Show the video version of a classic, then read the book and compare the two media. Use television as a catalyst to better understand newspaper and magazine articles on current events.

▶ **Discuss point of view.** Who's telling this story, whether it's a news report, a documentary, or a movie? How would it have been different if someone else — a different character, or the subject of the news story instead of the reporter — had told it?

▶ **Learn geography from TV.** Weather reports, news reports, documentaries, even sports all originate somewhere. Keep an atlas or globe near the TV set, and see where those places really are.

▶ **Set limits and stick to them.** Tell children they can watch a certain amount of television. Pull the plug if necessary.

former member of the National Commission on Excellence in Education, agrees that parents should monitor their child's homework. "Language barriers as well as levels of understanding, however, may diminish a parent's role," she cautions. Most schools now are trying to reach out to non-English speaking parents by providing interpreters or hiring staff who know other languages.

Parents can also teach their child how to set and achieve goals, which will help build confidence and self-esteem. One way is to teach children how to divide their time and assignments into manageable chunks. Another helpful practice is to have a child track his or her days to find ways of freeing up time for more studying or to better balance a schedule that might be too heavily weighted toward schoolwork or leisure. Children who are allowed to become involved in their own scheduling and goal setting become more self-reliant, and often more enthusiastic about studying.

10. Use the best of TV, then turn the rest off. Foster media skills.

Parents who go to the library don't let their children read any book that falls off the shelf, says Bobbi Kamil, executive director of Cable in the Classroom, a public service of the cable television industry supported by AASA and other national education groups. By the same token, parents and others shouldn't allow children to watch any program that comes on, Kamil adds.

Children can and do watch programs that support what they are learning in school. Programs such as "Sesame Street," "The Magic School Bus," and nature shows provide children with enjoyable learning experiences. Of course, much of what children view on a regular basis is inappropriate on many levels. Some programs may be too violent or sexually explicit, others may be too frightening, and many are simply mindless and waste a child's valuable time.

If parents watch television with their children, they can talk about the difference between reality and "make-believe." Children can be encouraged to learn about local, national, and world events and can use newspapers and magazines to gather even more information.

Watch for potholes on the information highway. Television isn't the only media culprit. "As the first travelers on the information superhighway, today's young people will be bombarded with a multitude of images," says Kamil. "Helping students deal with those images requires parents to become media literate." Issues already have been raised over whether children are able to access pornography or adult-only information and images on the Internet, CD-ROM, and other applications. In order to help students make the best use of today's technology, parents should stay informed about what their children can access, how much time they are spending on line, and why they are using such media outlets.

CHAPTER 4

Citizens and Government Working Together for the 21st Century

What Can Citizens Do to Prepare Students for the 21st Century?

1. Commit tax dollars as a long-term investment. View children as an investment, not a cost. Pay attention to how funding is being used.

2. Demonstrate that we, as a nation, value education and understand the relationship between education and a strong America.

3. Equalize funding, support, and opportunities.

4. Visit schools and become informed on issues. Influence schools by electing school leaders who care.

5. Set expectations for student results.

6. Extend schools into the community and value children.

7. Get involved in schools as volunteers, mentors, and role models for "at-risk" students.

We've got to help people understand the value of public education in this country. The quality of life for all of us is tied up in the quality of public education.

—Floretta Mckenzie, president, the McKenzie Group

"Citizens will need to make education a priority," says J.C. Sparkman, former executive vice president of Tele-Communications, Inc. "The fact that the majority of our school buildings were built between the late 1950s to mid-1960s indicates a major need to 'retool' and 'restructure' for the 21st century. This will require a real commitment from all stakeholders," he adds.

When asked what citizens and government would need to do to help prepare students for the 21st century, the responses were fairly consistent. For example, the Council of 55 emphasized that citizens and government must work together in key areas of funding, accountability, and involvement, *and* that they must see the powerful connection between education and a viable nation. "What made this country strong is public education," chief adviser and futurist Marvin Cetron, president of Forecasting International, emphasized.

Responses to both the citizens and government sections of our survey were similar. Therefore, we have listed those responses separately, but have combined similar items in our explanations.

What changes must citizens and government make, including those who have no children in school, to ensure our nation's children are prepared for the 21st century? The Council of 55 made several basic suggestions.

1. ***No. 1 for Citizens:*** **Commit tax dollars as a long-term investment. View children as an investment, not a cost. Pay attention to how funding is being used.** ***No. 2 for Government:*** **Commit funding for education.**

"One American mindset is that education is an expense in taxpayer dollars. We need to see children and youth as an investment," says Anne Campbell, a former member of the National Commission for Excellence in Education. "Taxpayers must understand the value of education," adds Christopher Cross, president of the Council for Basic Education.

Council members emphasized that citizens and their representatives in government on the local, state, and national levels need to understand the impact of education on communities throughout the nation. An indication of that impact is that high school graduates earn roughly twice as much as those who drop out of high school, and when higher salaries are translated into tax dollars and spendable income, they add up to more liveable communities and a stronger economy.

In a May 14, 1995 *New York Times* story, Labor Secretary Robert B. Reich was quoted as saying that "human capital is the nation's most precious asset," following the release of a study conducted by the Census Bureau for the U.S. Department of Education. The study, designed by the National Center of Educational Quality of the Workforce at the University of Pennsylvania, found that "increases in workers' education levels produce twice the gain in workplace efficiency as a comparable increase in the value of tools and machinery."

2. ***No. 2 for Citizens:*** **Demonstrate that we, as a nation, value education and understand the relationship between education and a strong America.**

Education is probably the single most important factor in whether an individual or nation succeeds, by almost any definition of success. As previously mentioned, studies by the U.S. Census Bureau and other organizations have shown that people's earning power increases significantly the more education they have. Educated people also tend to have more fulfilling lives, enriched by an appreciation for the arts, history, world affairs, science, and more.

Education helps us compete in the global economy. While the United States was once the leader in business and industry, countries such as Japan, Germany, Korea, and others are producing products that compare favorably to our own.

Preserving our democracy. School is where children usually learn about the Constitution and the Declaration of Independence, as well as other standards, laws, and principles that support our free and democratic society. The very fact that public education serves all children is symbolic of the nation's commitment to democracy. Our democratic process, including voting for elected officials, is founded on the assumption of an educated populace.

3. *No. 3 for Citizens:* **Equalize funding, support, and opportunities.**
   No. 1 for Government: **Equalize funding to ensure education for all of America's children.**

Equity in funding and educational opportunities has become an ongoing quest in states across the nation. Since the 1970s, more than 30 state Supreme Court decisions have been made addressing school finance cases.

The issue is complicated. Governors and state legislators tend to limit the impact of court orders and shy away from raising taxes when elections are being held. Citizens themselves sometimes object to higher taxes, or to giving up funds from wealthier areas to benefit those that are poorer. This is why, as efforts move forward to equalize, attention needs to be focused on sources of revenue and the adequacy of funding. Unless all factors are considered, schools and school systems stand a good chance of being leveled down rather than being leveled up.

Thoughtful citizens must constantly challenge their elected and appointed leaders to ensure that each and every child has a shot at the brass ring, whether the child's community is rich, poor, or somewhere in between.

"Federal and state government have a role in ensuring equal access and opportunity," says Floretta McKenzie, president of the McKenzie Group and former superintendent of the Washington, D.C., public schools. "The federal government must be diligent in making sure that every citizen has the opportunity for quality education."

4. *No. 4 for Citizens:* **Visit schools and become informed on issues.**
   Influence schools by electing school leaders who care.

"If primary and secondary education are to gain any kind of integral value by the time we reach the 21st century, parents, alumni, neighborhood businesses, and political institutions all must be brought into its processes," says George C. Lodge, author of *Work in the 21st Century: An Anthology of Writings on the Changing World of Work.* "Students must be allowed to see, in fact, that all of these institutions contribute to life and that students can contribute to the institutions—that the student can make a difference."

The Council of 55 suggested many ways community members and government can support schools. Among them:

- Elect and appoint school leaders who truly care about children and education.
- Pay attention to school issues and find out how you can help.
- Ask school leaders what kind of financial and other support they need to be successful in educating students, and then provide it.
- Visit schools as often as possible, and volunteer to help.

Citizens need to get involved not only by investing in children through tax dollars but also by stepping forward as volunteers, mentors, and role models for students, including those who might be at risk of failure. Equally important, citizens should be informed about issues affecting their community and elect school board members who will work collaboratively with local educators to create a positive learning experience for children.

Many schools open their facilities for community education programs and serve as sites for job training or retraining, as well as for child care, which soon may extend to elder care. Each school is and will likely become even more of a community center as more people work at home and seek a common place to meet and learn.

"We need to extend learning into the community," says Stephanie Pace Marshall, executive director of the Illinois Mathematics and Science Academy. In the future, schooling may extend even further beyond currently defined age groups and far outside the walls of the local school. We can expect that schools will draw larger circles that bring even more people in.

"Interested citizens must recognize that the schools face a quadrilateral dilemma. The schools are but one component of a grand system linking the home, church, and government," says author Donald C. Orlich in his *Education Digest* article, "Social Challenges to America 2000." According to Orlich, "the church provides moral, religious, ethical, and philosophical elements. The home provides support, nurturing, self-esteem, confidence, and caring. The school assumes the role of providing formal education and extending the core ideals of home and church. The government provides the legal and financial support."

Society's mirror. However, our Council of 55 questioned the evolving roles of both home and school, recognizing that schools have become increasingly responsible not only for educating youth, but for addressing the social, welfare, and economic ills of our society, as mentioned in previous chapters. "Schools of any society mirror that society," says Orlich. This is especially relevant in looking at the dilemmas facing American society in the 1990s.

Paul Houston, executive director of the American Association of School Administrators, has noted that "while it may take a whole village to educate a child, in some cases, the village itself is broken." Whatever the state of society, schools still are viewed as having primary responsibility in preparing young people for the future.

5. *No. 5 for Citizens:* **Set expectations for student results.** *No. 5 for Government:* **Develop standards for accountability.**

The close of the 20th century saw an increasing focus on standards. In education, standards were being developed by curriculum organizations, professional groups, and local school systems, with support from states and the federal government, all in the interest of better education. The standards movement has stirred heated debate, with some fearing that national standards could lead to a national curriculum that would undermine state and/or local control of schools.

Eight national education goals have generally been well accepted. However, those goals have spurred efforts to develop standards that would further define them and determine whether communities, schools, and students are reaching them.

Forecaster Marvin Cetron sees education institutions paying more attention to the outcomes and effectiveness of their programs. In "An American Renaissance in the Year 2000," Cetron predicts that the public and state legislatures will increasingly demand an assessment of student achievement and hold schools accountable. In addition, Cetron sees more states looking to the national education goals to assess their schools' performance.

Stephen Kleinsmith, director of Secondary Education for the Millard Public Schools in Omaha, Nebraska, says, "We must require set learning standards for students." He adds, "We need standards of accountability for parents, school leaders, and teachers as well."

Cautions Campbell, "All students can learn and will learn, but they learn differently in response to their style, interest, and desires." Accepting that children learn information at an individual pace, many school districts throughout the nation are shifting from time-based learning to performance-centered learning. Instead of basing a child's education on how much "time" he or she has spent in a specific class, performance is being evaluated based on the knowledge gained or skills acquired.

Some members of the Council of 55 noted that:

➡ Increased expectations may require additional time for learning.

➡ To be successful, schools may need to pay more attention to student learning styles.

➡ Accomplishing higher expectations may require some political decisions, such as lengthening the school day or year, devoting more resources to educational research, and eliminating laws and rules that inhibit schools from taking bold steps.

In "Will 21st-Century Schools Really Be Different?" Linda Darling-Hammond notes that while accountability will be one key area of school reform, it is changing, as schools move toward performance-centered education measured by performance-based testing. Schools today are engaged in much more useful forms of student and school assessment, pointed at higher-order thinking and performance skills, she says. They use research, projects, portfolios, exhibitions, debates, inquiries, and peer- and self-evaluation, along with students' public defense of their work and ideas.

"These strategies allow students to display not only what they know, but what they can do. Evaluation is by the progress they make, not by being compared to others," Darling-Hammond notes. In 10 content areas, including the arts, civics/government, English, foreign languages, geography, history, math, physical education/health, science, and social studies, national associations are working together to develop subject-matter standards as guidelines for classroom teachers.

6. *No. 6 for Citizens:* **Extend schools into the community and value children.**

By becoming the hub of a community, a school sends a message to parents and other citizens that it values children. "This is of vital political importance as the population ages and smaller numbers of citizens have their own kids in school," said one council member.

Schools can make themselves more intrinsic to community life by offering such services as adult learning classes, the use of computers after school hours (this also may be one way schools can pay for their own technology—by charging a small fee for adult learners to use the school facilities), offering athletic facilities, and more.

Child care programs are offered at many schools and elder care programs may be coming soon as the baby boom generation ages.

Still other programs are targeted at at-risk populations. For example, the Citizen Education Center and the Washington State Migrant Council offer a literacy program for Mexican immigrant farm workers. The program features instruction in English as a second language, early childhood education, and parent education classes.

Demand for education and training will strain resources as enrollments in the nation's schools grow beyond 50 million students around the turn of the century.

Community education may expand as growing numbers of people working at home or needing to update their skills look to school facilities as satellite campuses of two- and four-year colleges.

The bond between schools and communities will strengthen, and as our society prepares students for the 21st century, it will likely find that those students are of all ages. Politically, educators will need to inform, involve, and serve even more people beyond "school age," since growing numbers of homes no longer have students in school.

We need to value our children. Echoing the Council of 55, AASA Executive Director Paul Houston emphasizes the need for our nation to value children.

In addressing the 1995 AASA National Conference on Education, Houston expressed alarm that in the richest nation on earth, one child in four lives in poverty. Parents, he said, spend 40 percent less time with their children than parents did in 1965. He expressed sadness and outrage at the fact that "since 1988, teenage boys are more likely to die from gunshot wounds than from all other natural causes combined."

Houston called on school leaders to "articulate the needs of children to the greater community, since our children too often have no voice in our society." He also recommended a Children's Investment Trust, a program similar to Social Security, which would devote specified tax dollars to children and youth; a greater commitment to ensuring children's rights; and a Shepherd's Program to remind all citizens of the important roles they must play in nurturing children, who are the future.

7. *No. 7 for Citizens:* **Get involved in schools as volunteers, mentors, and role models for "at risk" students.**

At-risk children and youth need role models. That's why it is important for adult volunteers to serve as mentors for young people who need added attention.

A 1992 book, *At-Risk...Families and Schools Becoming Partners,* published by the ERIC Clearinghouse on Educational Management, makes the argument that at-risk children usually come from home environments very different from school. The book quotes author Sara Lawrence Lightfoot, who notes that children are confused by the dichotomy. "The predictable consequence in such situations is that children usually embrace the familiar home culture and reject the unfamiliar school culture, including its academic components and goals," she writes.

Community members can help bridge the gap between the home and school environments by serving as tutors, speaking in schools on careers or life experiences, acting as "Big Brothers" or "Big Sisters," working with academic or sport clubs, and more. In all of these instances, adults serve as positive role models that children may or may not encounter at home. In fact, when adults volunteer in schools, all students benefit, not just those at risk.

8. *No. 3 for Government:* **Support professional development for teachers and administrators.**

Throughout this study, members of the Council of 55 emphasized that education may be blessed with dozens of tools, from computers to television. However, students are taught and schools and school systems are operated by professionals whose need for continuing professional development must be met.

Said one member of the council, "Without teacher-guided self-improvement incentives and a greater investment in staff development, no meaningful improvement will ever occur or be sustained." Members of the council called upon state and federal government to provide resources that support needed professional development for both teachers and administrators.

Goals 2000

On the national level, Congress adopted eight national goals for education. The Goals 2000: Educate America Act was a bipartisan agreement that we must improve education so that American students will be prepared for the challenges facing them in the 21st century. Through Goals 2000, states and local school districts can apply for federal funds to help improve education. An 18-member National Education Goals Panel, comprised of governors, state legislators, members of Congress, and two individuals appointed by the president, is responsible for reporting progress toward reaching national education goals. In addition, the Panel approves criteria for developing standards for higher education and serves as a review board for the voluntary standards on curriculum content and student performance.

By the year 2000 in the United States:

1. All children will start school ready to learn.

2. The high school graduation rate will increase to at least 90 percent.

3. All students will leave grades 4, 8, and 12 having demonstrated competency over challenging subject matter, including English, mathematics, science, foreign languages, civics and government, economics, arts, history and geography. Every school will ensure that all students learn to use their minds well, so they are prepared for responsible citizenship, further learning, and productive employment in our nation's modern economy.

4. The nation's students will be the first in the world in mathematics and science achievement.

5. Every adult will be literate and possess the knowledge and skills necessary to compete in a global economy and exercise the rights and responsibilities of citizenship.

6. Every school will be free of drugs, violence, firearms, and alcohol and will offer a disciplined environment conducive to learning.

7. Teachers will have access to programs to improve their professional skills and acquire the knowledge and skills necessary to instruct and prepare all students for the next century.

8. Every school will promote partnerships to increase parental involvement and participation in promoting the social, emotional, and academic growth of children.

9. *No. 4 for Government:* Refrain from unfunded mandates.

Another significant concern of the Council of 55 is frustration over unfunded mandates.

If programs are required by state or federal government, they should also be funded at the level specified in the laws or regulations, and educators should be consulted as those laws or regulations are conceived and developed.

"All they (unfunded mandates) do is raise expectations unreasonably. They are, in many ways, cruel hoaxes that don't come to fruition," said a member of the Council. However, another Council member countered, "The mandates wouldn't be there if we were doing the job."

10. *No. 6 for Government:* **Provide incentives for promoting innovation.**

Members of the council called on federal, state, and local government to provide resources for innovation. Those incentives range from research and recognition to actual dollars. (See Goals 2000 sidebar on p. 58 for one example.)

11. *No. 7 for Government:* **Structure research to match current and future needs.**

Members of the Council of 55 called on state and federal government to support significant research focusing "on the fundamentals of learning and teaching."

For decades, educators have decried the lack of funds devoted to educational research, especially when compared to investments in R&D made by business and industry. They have also called upon government to consult with local educators, those closest to children, to determine what types of research would be most helpful to them.

"Government is another critical area that must be restructured. Policy, in many instances, stands in the way of some of the innovative strategies that have been mentioned here," says J.C. Sparkman.

In our next chapter, we'll explore what the Council of 55 suggests business and professional people can do to support education.

Business and Professional Leaders: Partners in Preparing Students for the 21st Century

What Can Business, Industry, and Professional Leaders Do To Prepare Students for the 21st Century?

1. Support taxes for education.
2. Develop flexible company policies that encourage employee involvement in schools.
3. Offer to share resources.
4. Develop partnerships with education.
5. Get involved in education as an example of leadership.
6. Demonstrate the value of education by hiring only competent workers.
7. Elevate the status of teaching and education.
8. Model moral and ethical behavior.

We need to stop educating people as if they'll have a plant to run when they graduate.

— Jennifer James, cultural anthropologist

Businesses' interest in the success or failure of public schools intensified around World War I, when Americans became concerned about producing workers able to compete in the world marketplace. Since then, business interest in education has ebbed and flowed, following fluctuations in the economy and the need for an even more skilled work force.

However, since the publication of *A Nation at Risk* in 1983, the business community at large has kept a close eye on public schools' ability to equip students with the skills, knowledge, and behaviors needed to be successful in the world of work.

This increased attention and involvement has not always been met with universal approval. Some express concern that the role of education must be broader than just providing people who are employable. Others caution that some businesses are using schools for commercial purposes as a marketplace for their products and services. Still, business involvement, properly planned and managed, can be beneficial to all.

Are Students Ready for the Future?

In its technology plan, the Michigan State Board of Education notes:

> There is a growing mismatch between the literacy of the work force and job skill requirements. The cost of an under-skilled or unqualified work force to society and industry grows greater every year. In 1990, business spent nearly $25 billion on basic skills training for new workers.

Business, labor, the schools, and the nation all need to reflect on how well they are positioned to meet the increasingly higher level skills and education required by the jobs of the future. It is estimated that 80 percent of the jobs that will exist in the year 2000 do not exist today.

Authors Sue E. Berryman and Thomas R. Bailey, in *The Double Helix of Education and the Economy*, state: "The workplace is changing and these changes are gradually rendering education as traditionally delivered more and more unconnected to what its graduates need to know and how they need to perform at work."

Moreover, the 1990 report, "America's Choice: High Skills or Low Wages," by the National Center on Education and the Economy's Commission on the Skills of the American Workforce, argues that it is not only skills, but sound ethics that will characterize the valued employee of the future. "The primary concern of more than 80 percent of employers was finding workers with a good work ethic and appropriate social behavior: 'reliable,' 'a good attitude,' 'a pleasant appearance,' 'a good personality,'" the report notes. (See Chapter 1, behaviors section, page 20.)

High tech machinery has replaced many steady assembly line jobs, and workers are more and more called on to trouble-shoot and analyze systems

APPRENTICESHIPS AND VOCATIONAL EDUCATION

Because the United States lacks a national system to move young people from school into the workplace, an interest in apprenticeships has emerged, according to authors Sue Berryman and Thomas Bailey in a 1992 publication, *The Double Helix of Education and the Economy*. "A work-based system, therefore, has seemed a good solution, simultaneously eliminating the problem of coordinating work-oriented schooling with the workplace and reducing any school-to-work transition problems for youth." One recommendation Berryman and Bailey suggest is to "organize learning around the principles of cognitive apprenticeship," which "stresses subject-specific content and the learning strategies and skills required to operate effectively in, on, and with the content." This is designed to create a well-prepared mind at ease with the demands of real-world tasks and equipped to continue learning. In "Hands and Minds: Redefining Success in Vocational Technical Education," education writer Linda Chion-Kenney notes that "what is needed, some educators say, is a marriage—not sibling rivalry—between academic and vocational education; between theory and practice; between using your mind and testing your talents in both chalk-and-talk and hands-on learning environments."

for efficiency. Today's students, then, must be well-versed in higher order skills needed for such work, and be comfortable with technology.

Schools must also prepare students to compete on the international marketplace with such technological giants as Japan and Germany.

Businesses, then, only help themselves by playing a leading role in supporting the transformation of schools.

Futurist Marvin Cetron, president of Forecasting International and a chief advisor for *Preparing Students for the 21st Century*, predicts that more businesses will form partnerships with schools and offer job training programs. He also stresses a need for America to strengthen vocational education and remove what some feel is a negatively stereotyped avenue for students not on the college track.

A different view. Some believe schools are doing fairly well in preparing the nation's youth for future employment. In "The Myth of Public School Failure," Richard Rothstein emphasizes that public schools now produce students possessing most academic skills currently demanded by employers. He cites a survey conducted in 1989 by The Commission on the Skills of the American Workforce, which found that "more than 80 percent of American employers were satisfied with new hires' education."

Rothstein suggests improved apprenticeship and workplace training as one reform that could work. "Schools presently send students with adequate numeric and literary skills into the workforce. Work habits may not be adequate," however, he adds. "Curricular reforms should emphasize team building and cooperative skills."

What Can Business Leaders Do?

When asked what support business, industry, and professional leaders need to provide to ensure that students are prepared for the 21st century, the Council of 55 suggested:

1. Support taxes for education.

Educators become alarmed when business people and others make public statements about the need for education to improve, then turn around and lobby against taxes to support those improvements. Unfunded mandates have drained many school systems of precious funds needed to improve student achievement.

Education is an investment, not an expense. Therefore, businesspeople should realize that an investment in education pays off in many ways: a better educated workforce, a better quality of life in the community, and a future market for products and services. Educated people often make more money and will have more spendable income to buy products and services tomorrow.

Businesses can help in this area by supporting local school budgets and levies, and lobbying on the local, state, and national levels for more adequate education funding. Shortchanging education may save a few tax dollars in the short run, but in the long run may be the most expensive dollars ever saved.

2. Develop flexible company policies encouraging employee involvement in schools.

As the number of two-career and single-parent families increases and as society grows to appreciate the importance of community involvement in schools, businesses are becoming more flexible in allowing parents and others to incorporate school involvement into the work day. Some ideas for business expressed by the Council of 55 include:

➡ Provide paid time off for parent/teacher conferences, similar to time off to vote.

➡ Offer opportunities for employees to visit their child's school.

➡ Run for the local school board or encourage employees to do so.

➡ Give employees some time off to tutor a student or speak to a class. Students need to see the connection between what they are learning in school and its application in the world of work.

"In looking at several reports, it seems that education and the family are not held in high regard. Business, industry, and professional leaders all talk the talk, but they don't walk the walk," says Richard Warner, a member of the Council of 55 and principal of Fargo South High School in Fargo, North Dakota. Warner suggests that funding for education, sound family leave policies, and providing employees time to volunteer in schools are a few ways businesspeople could help. "We are low on the list of industrialized countries that support education and the family," Warner adds.

The benefits of employee involvement are mutual: Businesses that promote the importance of parental

---

WHAT IS "QUALITY" VOCATIONAL-TECHNICAL EDUCATION?

According to The National Council on Vocational Education, "quality" vocational-technical education is essential in providing the work force the United States must have to be internationally competitive. In essence, a quality vocational-technical program:

▶ Establishes a close working relationship with business/industry.

▶ Hires instructors who have had experience in the business and industry that they are teaching.

▶ Integrates vocational student organizations into the classroom.

▶ Integrates academic and vocational-technical education concepts.

▶ Coordinates secondary and postsecondary vocational-technical education programs.

▶ Makes a commitment to career awareness and planning for students.

▶ Has access to and coordinates with a modern technology education component.

▶ Gives students opportunities to develop critical-thinking, problem-solving, and teamwork skills, and a commitment to lifelong learning, especially self-teaching.

▶ Uses an ongoing evaluation procedure to constantly improve the program and ensure that it is teaching the skills and competencies that employers need.

involvement and that support families tend to increase employee motivation and satisfaction, notes Janet Cox, director of communications and member services for the National Association for Partners in Education.

3. Offer to share resources.

While financial resources are appreciated, companies also may want to encourage schools to bring classes in for field trips, donate computers or other equipment, allow adults to use technology or other services, counsel on business matters, and more.

Some businesses open their own staff training to educators who want to learn applicable skills such as team building, shared decision making, or other practices, according to Cox. Or, a company might host a school's cafeteria staff for instruction in inventory and management practices, for example.

"There is a lot of pressure for schools to meet quality standards," Cox adds. Businesses are attuned to competition and customer service, and schools can benefit from this expertise.

4. Develop partnerships with education.

"Business and industry can be instrumental in guiding education toward future employment needs," according to one member of the Council of 55. A school-business partnership, like any partnership, implies mutual benefits and responsibilities. Partnerships often result in the mutual sharing of information, ideas, time, money, and support. Schools benefit through acquiring needed financial resources, opportunities for staff and student training, and additional positive role models for students.

Conversely, businesses can become actively involved in "what schools teach and how they teach it," says Cox. One reason to become involved at the decision-making level is that businesses can be instrumental in raising the quality of their own entry level employees. Businesses have important contributions to make in improving both the quality and relevance of vocational education and career education programs, as well. Businesspeople can provide a direct link to the reality of the workplace.

Reaching a higher plane. Schools and businesses need to work together in common purpose to improve life in the community. This is the direction school-business partnerships are taking, according to Cox. While both still value one-on-one mentoring and guest speakers, relationships between businesses and schools are evolving along a "partnership continuum" that is characterized by increased business influence on school boards, education advocacy at the state level, and collaborations with social service agencies to meet the needs of the broader community.

Schools play a pivotal role in making a community attractive to present and future employers and employees and in increasing the community brain trust.

THE SCHOOL-TO-WORK OPPORTUNITIES INITIATIVE

"A real recognition and concern exists about the difficult transition that faces all high school graduates as they prepare to live on their own, assume new roles in the adult community, and enter the world of work," write authors Fred Krieg, Peg Brown, and John Ballard in *Transition: School to Work*. In 1994 it was estimated that 3.4 million, or 11 percent of 16- to 24-year-olds, did not have a high school diploma, nor were they currently in school. When these students are added to the large number of students who possess a degree but few marketable skills, it was speculated that a large population is entering the workforce unprepared for the demands of the 21st century.

The School-to-Work Opportunities Act of 1994 was designed to provide all students equal access to work-based and school-based learning through linkages between secondary and postsecondary education and employers. The legislation puts in place a transition system to ease students' passage between school and work by offering programs that combine learning in real work settings with learning in the school. Basically, students declare a major or area of specialization and earn credits toward a skill certificate, which indicates the student has mastered skills at levels endorsed by the National Skill Standards Board. "Work experience is to be mentored, and instruction is to include workplace competencies, positive work attitudes, and to the extent practicable, all aspects of the student's chosen career field," according to Krieg, Brown, and Ballard.

The act also provides follow-up by helping students find jobs or get additional training. The legislation invites communities to work together to build a system that will create a path students can follow from school to a good first job or to further education and training. Communities are encouraged to apply for grants in the areas of development, implementation, local partnership and high-poverty areas to help states and localities build their own school programs.

5. Get involved in education as an example of leadership.

Businesses are more attractive to potential customers when they demonstrate their social responsibility. A business that visibly and with enthusiasm invests in children, family, and schools, sends a message loud and clear that it cares about the future of the community and its customers.

Business leaders can demonstrate their community leadership on behalf of education by becoming school board members, mentors, internship supervisors, and classroom guests who show the connection between what is learned in school and life in the business and professional world.

6. Demonstrate the value of education by hiring only competent workers.

When businesses announce that they need people who have done well in school, who have studied hard and developed their knowledge and skills, yet have no jobs for them, students become cynical. How well students do in school, coupled with the ability to do the job, should be a prime factor in hiring.

If businesses do not stress the value of school achievement and effort, then students perceive education to be of lesser value and may not apply themselves. If students do not see an economic advantage as well as advantages in their civic and personal lives from getting a good education, business and industry lose out.

Businesses must do more, including holding kids accountable for their school performance and attendance.

7. Help to elevate the status of teaching and education.

Many believe that people in other countries treat educators more professionally and hold them in higher esteem than we do in this country.

From the public platform to hiring practices, education and educators need public support, including support from the business community. Such support can take various forms: CEOs and others can visit classrooms to give presentations on how they attained their positions. Business leaders can speak on practical applications of schoolwork —how lessons learned in school are used day to day. Schools and businesses can work together to develop internships for teachers so that they can have firsthand knowledge of the working world and speak to students from experience.

8. Model moral and ethical behavior.

Concern about values and ethics emerged in nearly every area of this study.

Children and youth learn from examples they see around them, from

THE SCANS REPORT

In 1991, a commission headed by former U.S. Secretary of Labor Lynn Martin, the Secretary's Commission on Achieving Necessary Skills (SCANS) conducted a watershed study of business needs that sounded an urgent cry to revamp our schools to equip students with what they would need to know and do to be prepared for the future.

The commission, which included representatives of education, government, business, and labor unions, concluded that students today and in the future will need radically different skills than they possessed in the past.

Briefly, the report concluded:

▶ All American high school students must develop a new set of competencies and foundation skills if they are to enjoy a productive, full, and satisfying life.

▶ The qualities of high performance that today characterize our most competitive companies must become the standard for the vast majority of our companies, large and small, local and global.

▶ The nation's schools must be transformed into high-performance organizations in their own right.

This first report, "What Work Requires of Schools: A SCANS Report for America 2000," was followed by other reports from the Commission such as the "Skills and Tasks for JOBS: A SCANS Report for America 2000." The latter lists specific careers and the skills individuals need to be successful in those jobs. These SCANS reports should be considered by school district leaders, school-to-work administrators, vocational instructors and others to ensure students are going in the right direction to be in a good position to get and keep good jobs.

WORKPLACE KNOW-HOW

The know-how identified by SCANS is made up of five competencies and a three-part foundation of skills and personal qualities that are needed for solid job performance. These include:

COMPETENCIES
Effective workers can productively use:

- **Resources** — allocating time, money, materials, space, and staff.
- **Interpersonal Skills** — working on teams, teaching others, serving customers, leading, negotiating, and working well with people from culturally diverse backgrounds.
- **Information** — acquiring and evaluating data, organizing and maintaining files, interpreting and communicating, and using computers to process information.
- **Systems** — understanding social, organizational, and technological systems, monitoring and correcting performance, and designing or improving systems.
- **Technology** — selecting equipment and tools, applying technology to specific tasks, and maintaining and troubleshooting technologies.

THE FOUNDATION
Competence requires:

- **Basic Skills** — reading, writing, mathematics, speaking, and listening.
- **Thinking Skills** — thinking creatively, making decisions, solving problems, seeing things in the mind's eye, knowing how to learn, and reasoning.
- **Personal Qualities** — individual responsibility, self-esteem, sociability, self-management, and integrity.

Source: What Work Requires of Schools: A SCANS Report for America 2000, The Secretary's Commission on Achieving Necessary Skills, U.S. Department of Labor, 1991, p. vii.

their parents, teachers, friends, public officials, entertainers, and business people, to name a few. Unfortunately, young people take lessons from what some perceive as a "win however you can so long as you can get away with it" society.

Members of the Council of 55 noted that while schools have an important impact on children as they learn about codes of ethics, for example, adults in the community and in the nation set an example for them in the way they treat each other and the way they do business.

Building Effective School-Business Partnerships

Like any worthwhile endeavor, the most successful school-business partnerships are well planned and include an evaluation mechanism. Schools might consider the following when developing and implementing partnerships:

- Research interested businesses to make sure their management, products, motivations, and goals are ethical.
- Identify the benefits to be gained by the various participants.
- Involve those closest to the work in the decision making.
- Ensure that all children have equal access to opportunities afforded by businesses.
- Provide needed training.
- Communicate with the community about any school-business partnerships.

Catching the Dreams of Tomorrow

Native Americans artistically craft dream catchers from wood, feathers, stones, shells, and leather. Circular in shape, it is believed these dream catchers capture both good and bad dreams and funnel the good dreams through the center hole to the sleeper. Bad dreams become enmeshed in the intricate webbing and perish in the light of day. Because it is believed that dreams can change or direct one's path in life, dreams attain a magical status.

As we look toward a new millennium, parents, educators and schools, citizens, government and business have an opportunity to be the weaver of dreams for our children's future. By surrounding our students with a circle of support and a consistent message emphasizing education and lifelong learning, we can better prepare our students for the 21st century, and for a lifetime of success.

References

Academe Gets Lessons From Big Business." *The Wall Street Journal.* December 15, 1992, p. B1.

Adler, Mortimer J. *The Paideia Proposal: An Educational Manifesto.* New York: Macmillan, 1982.

American Federation of Teachers, the Educational Excellence Network, and Freedom House. *Education for Democracy.* 1987.

"A Nation at Risk: The Imperative for Education Reform." National Commission on Excellence in Education, 1983.

Au, Kathryn. "Issue." *ASCD Update* 36, 5 (June 1994): 7.

Barton, P.; and Coley, R. *America's Smallest School: The Family.* Princeton: Policy Information Center, Educational Testing Service, 1992.

Bates, Percy. "Science Education and Equity." *Equity Coalition.* III, 2 (Fall 1993-Spring 1994): 1 & 29.

Berryman, Sue E.; and Bailey, Thomas R. *The Double Helix of Education and the Economy.* New York: The Institute on Education and the Economy, Columbia University Teachers College, 1992.

Boyer, Ernest. *High School: A Report on Secondary Education in America.* The Carnegie Foundation for the Advancement of Teaching. New York: Harper and Row, Publishers, 1983.

Cetron, Marvin. "An American Renaissance In The Year 2000 — 74 Trends That Will Affect America's Future — and Yours." *The Futurist.* 28 (March 1994) SS1-SS11.

Chion-Kenney, Linda. *Hands and Minds: Redefining Success in Vocational Technical Education.* Washington, D.C.: Education Writers Association and William T. Grant Foundation Commission on Youth and America's Future, 1992.

Darling-Hammond, Linda. "Will 21st-Century Schools Really Be Different?" *The Education Digest* (September 1994): 4-8.

Darling-Hammond, Linda. *Technos,* 3, 2 (Summer 1994): 6-9.

De Souza, Anthony R. "Time for Geography: The New National Standards." Geography for Life — Widening Student Horizons for The 21st Century. *NASSP Bulletin* 78, 564 (October 1994): 1.

"The Duty of Civility." *Royal Bank Letter*, 76, 3 (May/June 1995): Royal Bank of Canada: 1-2.

Franks, Lucinda. "Little Big People." *The New York Times Magazine*. 28 (October 10, 1993).

"Getting Tough." *Time Magazine*. (February 1, 1988): p. 54.

"Helping Students Resolve Conflict." *ASCD Update* (December 1993): p.4.

Hodgkinson, Harold. "A Demographic Look At Tomorrow." Washington, D.C.: Institute for Educational Leadership. 1992.

Houston, Paul D. "Winning the Race with the Clock or Postcards from the Edge." Speech made at the Southwest Regional Laboratory Conference, Long Beach, Calif., 1991.

Kids Count Data Book 1993, Greenwich, Conn.: The Annie E. Casey Foundation and Center for the Study of Social Policy, 1993.

Linn, Eleanor. "Science and Equity: Why This Issue Is Important." *Equity Coalition*. III, 2 (Fall 1993-Spring 1994): 3.

Lodge, George C. *Work in the 21st Century: An Anthology of Writings on the Changing World of Work*. Alexandria: American Society for Personnel Administration, 1994.

Mathews, Jay. "Odd Jobs." *The Washington Post*, August 13, 1995, P. H5.

Miller, Edward. "Letting Talent Flow: How Schools Can Promote Learning for the Sheer Love of It." *Harvard Education Letter*, X, 2 (March/April 1994).

O'Neil, John. "Rewriting the Book on Literature." *ASCD Curriculum Update* (June 1994): 1.

Oregon Schools for the 21st Century, The 1993-1994 Report Card. Oregon Department of Education, 1994.

Orlich, Donald C. "Social Challenges to America 2000." *The Education Digest* (March 1994): 4-6.

Prisoners of Time. A Report of the National Education Commission on Time and Learning. Washington, D.C.: U.S. Government Printing Office, 1994.

Ravitch, Diane. *The Troubled Crusade: American Education 1945-1980*. New York: Basic Books, Inc., 1983, pps. 47-48.

Rothstein, Richard. "The Myth of Public School Failure." *The American Prospect* (Spring 1993): 21-34.

Sivertsen, Mary Lewis. *Transforming Ideas for Teaching and Learning Science*. Washington, D.C.: U.S. Government Printing Office, 1993.

Stephens, Ann Bandy. "Increase the Peace. Skills for Resolving Conflicts." *Daily Press Newspapers in Education*, May 1983.

"Study Ties Education Gains To More Productivity Growth." *The New York Times*, May 14, 1995.

Transformation — What Minnesota Business Needs from Education. The Minnesota Business Partnership, 1993.

Council of 55

These individuals agreed to participate in the Delphi survey that produced this work. This does not necessarily mean they agreed with all conclusions discussed in this publication.

1. **Gordon Ambach**
   Executive Director
   Council of Chief State School
     Officers
   Washington, DC

2. **Tracey L. Bailey**
   1993 National Teacher of the Year
   Florida Department of Education
   Melbourne, FL

3. **Mary Bicouvaris**
   1989 National Teacher of the Year
   Associate Professor of Education
   Christopher Newport University
   Newport News, VA

4. **Judith Billings**
   Superintendent of Public Instruction
   State of Washington
   Olympia, WA

5. **Beverly Bjork**
   Director of Curriculum/Instruction
   Colorado Springs School District 11
   Colorado Springs, CO

6. **Anne Bryant**
   Executive Director
   American Association of University
     Women
   Washington, DC

7. **Don Cameron**
   Executive Director
   National Education Association
   Washington, DC

8. **Anne Campbell**
   Former Nebraska Commissioner
     of Education
   and former member of National
     Commission on Excellence in
     Education
   Lincoln, NE

9. **Gene Carter**
   Executive Director
   Association for Supervision and
     Curriculum Development
   Alexandria, VA

10. **Christopher Cross**
   President
   Council for Basic Education
   Washington, DC

11. **Tom Curley**
   President and CEO
   Gannett Company
   Arlington, VA

12. **Donald R. Draayer**
1990 National Superintendent
   of the Year
Former Superintendent
Minnetonka Public Schools
Excelsior, MN

13. **Jack Dulaney**
Superintendent
Monongalia County Schools
Morgantown, WV

14. **Tim Dyer**
Executive Director
National Association of Secondary
   School Principals
Reston, VA

15. **Arnold Fege**
Director of Governmental Relations
National PTA
Washington, DC

16. **Joseph Fernandez**
Executive Director
School Improvement Services, Inc.
Winter Park, FLA

17. **Howard Fuller**
Director
Institute for the Transformation of
   Learning
School of Education
Marquette University
Milwaukee, WI

18. **Mary Hatwood Futrell**
Dean
Graduate School of Education and
   Human Development
George Washington University
Washington, DC
Former NEA President

19. **Paul Goren**
Formerly of the National Governor's
Association
Executive Director
Policy and Strategic Services
Minneapolis Public Schools
Minneapolis, MN

20. **Lee Hager**
Assistant Superintendent
Curriculum & Instruction
Flagstaff Unified School District
Flagstaff, AZ

21. **Shirley J. Holloway**
Commissioner
Alaska State Department of
   Education
Juneau, AK

22. **John R. Hoyle**
Professor of Education
   Administration
Department of Education
   Administration
Texas A&M University
College Station, TX

23. **Jennifer James**
Cultural Anthropologist
Seahurst, WA

24. **Mary Jarvis**
Principal
Smoky Hill High School
Cherry Creek Public Schools
Aurora, CO

25. **Spike Jorgensen**
Former Superintendent
Alaska Gateway School District
Tok, AK

26. **Michael Kirst**
Professor
Stanford University
School of Education
Stanford, CA

27. **Stephen Kleinsmith**
Director of Secondary Education
Millard Public Schools
Omaha, NE

28. **K. Jessie Kobayashi**
Superintendent (Retired)
San Carlos, CA

29. **Joe Lopez**
Superintendent
Cuba Independent Schools
Cuba, NM

30. **Jose Tomas Maes**
Superintendent
Adams County School District # 1
Denver, CO

31. **Stephanie Pace Marshall**
Executive Director
Illinois Mathematics and Science
Academy
Aurora, IL

32. **Jean B. McGrew**
Superintendent
Northfield Township H.S.
District 225
Glenview, IL

33. **Kenneth Moffett**
1994 National Superintendent
of the Year
Superintendent
Lennox School District
Lennox, CA

34. **John Murphy**
Superintendent
Charlotte-Mecklenburg Schools
Charlotte, NC

35. **Frank Newman**
President
Education Commission of the States
Denver, CO

36. **Peggy Ondrovitch**
Superintendent
La Porte Community School District
La Porte, IN

37. **Carol Grosse Peck**
1991 National Superintendent
of the Year
Superintendent
Alhambra School District
Phoenix, AZ

38. **Bertha Pendleton**
Superintendent
San Diego U.S.D.
San Diego, CA

39. **Chris Pipho**
Division Director
Clearinghouse/State
Relations
Education Commission of the
United States
Denver, CO

40. **Carolyn Reedom**
Principal
Estes McDoniel School
Henderson, NV

41. **James Renier**
Chairman and CEO (Retired)
Honeywell, Inc.
Renier & Associates
Minneapolis, MN

42. **Rod Rice**
Executive Director
Buckeye Association of School
Administrators
Westerville, OH

43. **Victor Rodriguez**
Superintendent
San Antonio Independent School
District
San Antonio, TX

44. **Sam Sava**
Executive Director
National Association of Elementary
School Principals
Alexandria, VA

45. **Albert Shanker**
President
American Federation of Teachers
Washington, DC

46. **Thomas A. Shannon**
Executive Director
National School Boards Association
Alexandria, VA

47. **Paula Short**
Department of Educational
Administration
The Penn State University
College of Education
University Park, PA

48. **David Pearce Snyder**
Futurist
Bethesda, MD 20817

49. **J.C. Sparkman**
Former Executive Vice President
Executive Office
Tele-Communications, Inc. (TCI)
Englewood, CO

50. **Adam Urbanski**
President
Rochester Teachers Association/
    American Federation of Teachers
Rochester, NY

51. **Michael Usdan**
President
The Institute for Educational
    Leadership
Washington, DC

52. **Richard Warner**
Principal
Fargo South High School
Fargo, ND

53. **Sandra Welch**
Executive Vice President
Education Services
Public Broadcasting Service (PBS)
Alexandria, VA

54. **Karen Callison Woodward**
Superintendent
Anderson School District #5
Anderson, SC

55. **Larry Zenke**
Superintendent
Duval County Schools
Jacksonville, FL

Chief Advisers

Marvin Cetron
President
Forecasting International
Arlington, VA
Author of *Schools of the Future* and
    Educational Renaissance

Floretta McKenzie
President
The McKenzie Group
Washington, DC
Former superintendent
Washington, DC, Public Schools